SPORTSMAN'S BAG

Review Copy

SPORTSMAN'S BAG
By John Marchington.

Publication date:

13th October, 1975 at £4.50

*No review should appear before the date
of publication.*

*Photographs and biographical notes of authors
are usually available and will be supplied on
request to the Reviews Department.*

*Use of illustration material can also be
arranged.*

Faber & Faber

3 QUEEN SQUARE LONDON WC1N 3AU
Telephone: 01-278 6881

SPORTSMAN'S BAG

John Marchington

with photographs by the author
and line drawings by
Tom Banks

FABER & FABER · LONDON

First published in 1975
by Faber and Faber Limited
3 Queen Square London WC1
Printed in Great Britain by
Ebenezer Baylis and Son Limited,
The Trinity Press, Worcester, and London
All rights reserved

ISBN 0 571 10449 5

To my wife Janet

CONTENTS

ILLUSTRATIONS

*All photographs were taken by the author, except
for the jacket and plates 6 and 9 which were taken
by members of his family.*

ACKNOWLEDGEMENTS

Some of the photographs in this book have appeared previously in the *Shooting Times and Country Magazine* and *The Field,* and I am grateful to the Editors for their permission to reproduce them.

FOREWORD

John Marchington has made me think hard about my upbringing as a fisherman and shooter. Most people will have been introduced to the use of a shotgun or fishing rod through the enthusiasm of a close relative or friend. I was fortunate enough to owe my start with both to my father and under his tuition caught my first trout and shot my first rabbit. Later came many happy holidays with Jimmy Allison, keeper at Arbuthnott for forty years as was his father and grandfather before him! Forty years on now, I realize how very lucky I was to be born with the equivalent of the sportsman's silver spoon in my mouth. Nevertheless I later had to make the most of opportunities as they arose and, particularly during the war and immediate post-war period, first as a schoolboy, then a serviceman and finally an undergraduate, I learned the supreme satisfaction of searching for the chance to fish and shoot and of making each occasion a personal challenge.

Sporting memories of twenty-five and thirty years ago are one thing and the excitement of sporting occasions seldom vary but how much has changed since those earlier days. The opportunity to shoot and fish and learn the ways of wildlife has become the province of an ever widening circle of enthusiasts for whom John Marchington speaks most eloquently. Well endowed with all the necessary qualifications, he demonstrated his skill as an instructor in shooting lore and its application in his first shooting book *Shooting: A Complete Guide for Beginners* and now in *Sportsman's Bag*, although disclaiming any such intention, he has continued that process of instruction, with a wealth of personal anecdotes to spice a fund of knowledge and accomplishment of a comprehensive range of sporting experiences.

It is not only in his knack of adorning a tale but also the ability to explain what he did and how he does it that makes the book so valuable to fellow-sportsmen. This is no mere catalogue of sporting events or textbook pontifications! Few self-styled countrymen could equal the breadth of his achievement and fewer city-dwellers could emulate the determination and effort that must have gone into its attainment. It is one thing to talk about great days with rod and gun, when it is all laid on for you and a helpful guide is at your elbow all the time, and quite another to be able to tell of so much success and sheer enjoyment when all the skill has had to be mastered by yourself. John pays tribute to his mentors as is right but they would all feel the satisfaction of a job well done in reading of his unqualified zest for, and skill in, the sport in which he was instructed. We are all the wiser and the more fortunate that he has passed on their tuition to us, tempered by his own undoubted expertise.

This is a book for the enthusiastic country-lover and especially for those who like myself enjoy the anticipation of the stalk, the wait for flighting wildfowl or the cast and slow draw of the line through the water above all else that goes to make up the essence of the sporting scene. There is much to learn and even more to savour of that scene in these pages and I would like to wish this book and its author every success.

ARBUTHNOTT

INTRODUCTION

This book does not set out to instruct. In places it offers modest advice, but I can only describe it as a sporting hotch-potch—a patchwork quilt of memories, thoughts, advice and philosophies, sewn together with the twin threads of fishing and shooting. My justification for producing it is the enjoyment I hope it will give to my fellow sportsmen and the immense pleasure I have had in writing it.

My hope that it will be enjoyed is bolstered by the knowledge that, over the years, those books among the extensive literature of field sports which have endured are not those which set out to teach. The classics were written by men who could capture both the excitement of the chase and the beauty and atmosphere of the countryside. No angler can read Negley Farson's *Going Fishing* (*Country Life*) or Viscount Grey's *Fly Fishing* without an urge to fish and many a novice wildfowler first felt the call of the saltings in the pages of Peter Scott's *Morning Flight* (*Country Life*).

There are many other appealing books and, as the contents of this modest contribution began to evolve in my head, my mind returned constantly to the question of why such purely contemplative books are so attractive to sporting people. There is no denying that we who fish and shoot, and for that matter, hunt (although I know nothing of that sport), have a particular attachment to our pastimes. The reason, I am sure, lies in deep-rooted instincts. In the time-scale of the world it is only yesterday since we ran about in animal skins and lived in caves. The need to hunt to live held priority over all else for millions of years and the last couple of thousand has not erased it—merely covered it with a thin veneer of civilization. Once man lived outdoors and went in for shelter. Now we exist indoors and go out for fresh air. Only a handful of generations ago a man was his own butcher,

B
17

cook, house-builder, maker of light and heat and general provider of all things. Now we are specialists, each man with a special skill but relying on his, often unreliable, fellows for all else. It is an unnatural state and any activity that fulfils the faint urges from the mists of time gives pleasure. To sportsmen the greatest satisfaction comes from being outdoors with rod or gun, but when this is not possible we seek solace in tying a fly, polishing a gun stock, or the pages of a book. To this end I have attempted to capture with pen and camera some of the sights, sounds, moods and atmospheres of not only fishing and shooting but the countryside and the people who live in it. This is a book for people who love the touch of wind, rain and sun on their faces; people whose hearts leap at the thud of a taking salmon, or feel a quiver of excitement as a wigeon screaming down the wind folds to fast-flung barrels. It is equally for people who can lie in the heather watching a dragonfly dry its wings after a shower, or gain as much pleasure, between drives, talking to an elderly beater about horse ploughing as to a lunchtime neighbour about politics.

I hope that in its pages busy people may relax a little.

JOHN MARCHINGTON
Great Bookham
January 1974

CHAPTER ONE

GUNS, MEN AND PLACES

The violence associated with guns causes society to frown upon them and their ownership and their use carries a slight trace of guilt. My non-sporting friends who, although not fully understanding, appreciate and admire a new rod or a puppy, barely conceal their concern and disapproval when shown a new gun. It is therefore a pleasure to write on guns for a readership who will appreciate the satisfaction that comes from owning guns of character, though not necessarily of great value.

The peculiar satisfaction derived from a gun must owe much to the past, for from the beginning of time a man needed a weapon for food and protection. The Stone Age man with a particularly well-balanced club must have handled it with much the same satisfaction as I derive when, each August, I assemble my gun, mount it several times and run my hands over the cold metal and smooth wood. Countless men have gone through wars depending upon their guns for survival, and many others would have starved in desolate places but for their guns. The relationship of men with guns is so strongly woven with dramatic threads that the fascination is understandable.

Perhaps because of this background, guns—and the sport that goes with them—seem to attract colourful characters.

It is my good fortune to derive enormous pleasure and fun from observing my fellow humans and one does not have to be shooting for long to discover that both Guns (that is, the men) and guns (that is, the weapons) offer great variety. There are nasty cheap weapons and nasty cheap men; there are slow, heavy, big bores to be found in both varieties. Some are quick to fire and need only the merest touch to provoke an explosion; others need heavy provocation before they respond. There are treacherous guns and treacherous men; and sound, honest products, in both varieties, who will not let you down.

In the early years of one's shooting life success is all and the size of the bag usually determines the enjoyment of the day. It is the custom for those who have advanced beyond this stage to write loftily of the shallow standards of the young and philosophize on how time will teach them better values. The point so often forgotten is that the modest bag which the older man explains is quite sufficient for his pleasure would frequently represent a day of triumph for the beginner. I am inclined to hold forth on how a brace of grouse and a snipe is ample reward for a day on the hills and how my pleasure comes from the taste of clean air, etc. If I am honest I cast my mind back to the years when, as a teenager in Derbyshire, I would have been not just content but delirious with two grouse—the usual bag was nothing, and a couple of rabbits made it a day to be remembered. Certainly I do not belong among those elevated souls who claim indifference as to whether they shoot anything or not— for me shooting is a contest in which I pit my experience and skill against the quarry, and for full satisfaction, as they say in the cigarette advertisements, I must come home with something in the bag.

I appreciate a really fine gun but I have no great urge to own one, at least, that is, if I have to pay for it myself. Its very worth would be, I suspect, constantly inhibiting; a source of worry at every barbed-wire fence or passing shower. It might serve me better if all my shooting were done from a stationary position at driven game with a loader to wipe down the gun and case it after each drive, but without the variety of rough days on low and high ground, of wildfowling, sorties after pigeon and the other forms of shooting, I would enjoy my sport less.

No, the real value of a gun is not what it cost but the memories that go with it. When you have carried a gun through triumph and disaster; laid it by your side on the hill as you ate a knob of cheese and drank from a blue loch; or protected the action with your body, crouching in the lee of a hedge against a driving storm; cleaned it a thousand times; when the origin of each dent or blemish is known and recalls thoughts of people, places and good times past; then indeed it becomes a thing of value. The study in which I sit writing this is full of very valuable things; the primary feather of a golden eagle picked from the shore of a favourite loch; a corn dolly fashioned from straw from a Norfolk farm where I have had great sport; a gaff I made myself thirty years ago with metal traded from the blacksmith with a brace of rabbits ferreted from the Derbyshire hills; a thumb-stick which has helped me over hundreds of Hebridean miles; my daughters' first attempts at pottery. There are many other objects all of equally great value, and if the house burnt down tonight the insurance company would pay nothing for them.

It is reasonable to expect that a man could perform better with a very expensive gun than a cheap one but, in practice, I have reservations. The great point about the better gun is that it would be made to fit, but if the cheaper gun was of the same dimensions, or almost so, I doubt if there would be any real difference in results. Some years ago I was shooting on Skye when, moving too rapidly over seaweed-covered rocks, I dented the barrels of my gun so badly as to make it unusable. Feverish inquiry unearthed a local keeper's gun, unused for some years. It had begun life as a cheap Continental gun, probably some forty years earlier, and had deteriorated ever since. The barrels were rusty, inside and out. The action shook and the top lever, having a broken spring, flapped about loosely. There was insufficient cast-off and bend for me. I oiled it thoroughly, linked the top lever to the trigger guard with an elastic band and for the next ten days shot quite normally. It is possible that I might have hit an extra grouse or so with my own gun but I cannot be sure.

The first gun I recall was a cheap Belgian ·410 belonging to my Uncle Arthur. He and his brother Will farmed a couple of hundred acres of heavy land in central Norfolk and it was nearer to slavery than work. In the twenty-four years they spent there I never knew either of them take a day's holiday other than Christmas Day. Even the smallest pair of hands could be given work, so every school holiday I was packed off to Jordan Farm; willingly, I might add, for then, as now, I am only truly content when outdoors. Sunday, after the cows were milked (by hand, of course), and the other essential tasks of a mixed farm performed, Arthur would take a handful of the neat little dusky red cartridges, pick the ·410 from the corner in the barn and we would set off on the weekly shoot. To the spaniel and me it was heaven. I was about ten at the time and there could be no greater happiness. I can visualize Arthur now, picking his way furtively along a hedge-side, eyes flickering everywhere but never speaking a word; or standing stock-still in a gateway while the dog and I worked a hedge towards him. To me he seemed a marvellous shot although I doubt he had more than the average countryman's skill, which, contrary to legend, is not usually over-high. Certainly the little gun was excellent for the job of short-range snap shots, as rabbits bolted from clumps of thistles or pheasants showed for a brief second as they hurled themselves over the hedges.

At the other extreme the largest gun in whose company I had the honour of shooting in my early days was a single-barrel 8 bore, over five feet long. Its owner, Clive Minton, was then a Cambridge undergraduate, whose varied and extreme pursuits, ranging through wildfowling, netting birds for ringing and catching mallard on the Backs to appease his exceptional appetite, had earned him a reputation as an eccentric even in that miniature world of eccentrics. He it was who first took me wildfowling early one autumn, leading me onto the mudflats of The Wash wearing tennis shoes and a pair of shorts as if this was the natural way of things. We

spent many exciting nights subsequently, lying on the sea
wall waiting for the geese to flight in to feed under the moon.
I will always remember the great bowl of the sky, the frost on
the grass sparkling under the moon and the stirring of the sea.
We would wait, often for hours, and they were great times
for young men to think and talk about life. Philosophy comes
much easier under an open sky. Eventually from across the
sand and the mud would come a distant 'wink wink' and
numb, cold limbs would leap into action. If we had judged the
flight line correctly it was necessary only to stare into the sky
for the first suspicion of movement, but if the geese were
crossing to one side there would be a desperate rush along the
landward side of the wall, hampered by waders and heavy
clothing. I hold one marvellous memory of Clive silhouetted
against the moon with his monstrous 8 bore at the ready and
a spare cartridge clenched in his teeth for rapid reloading.
My own weapon was a superb 10 bore, double-barrel, hammer
gun by Tolley and my first pinkfoot fell to this in a copybook
setting under a Wash December moon. Nor did it fall to a
chance pellet for I found 13 B.Bs. in it. A feature of the old
hammer guns, unappreciated by modern sportsmen, is the
part played by the cocked hammers in aiming. It may be
fallacy but I felt, and others with whom I have talked share
the view, that framing the target between these 'horns'
encouraged the good practice of putting the barrels onto the
target from the moment mounting began. I still have the
Tolley—indeed, the dealer who sold it to me many years
back for £15 makes ever higher bids to regain it—and expect
to pass it on to my sons. It has been retired for some time,
but when I handle it I feel an urge, almost a duty, to take it
below the sea wall again.

My wildfowling days on The Wash began as the carefree
days of fowling in the area were ending and it is perhaps
worth recording the situation. Ever since sporting guns
evolved, The Wash provided unrestricted sport for all who
came. The arrival of the motor-car increased shooting pressures but The Wash was vast enough to absorb the extra
Guns. Further to the east, along the north Norfolk coast
where the fowl were more concentrated, the geese were

gradually driven away until, by the outbreak of the First World War, the wintering numbers were very small. With the end of the war came prosperity, more cheap mass-produced cars, and many more shooting-men looking for sport. The result was an invasion which led to ridiculous numbers of fowlers each week-end and some deplorable conduct. The main focal point was Shep White's, an old cottage lying under the sea wall north of Holbeach, once the home, obviously enough, of a shepherd called White but by then derelict. I slept rough in it on several occasions, waiting for the dawn, and preferring it to the old concrete pill box nearby, where a fowler once asphyxiated himself by lighting a stove and blocking the entrance to keep the heat in. After flight on a Sunday morning it was common to see anything from thirty to fifty cars at this one point alone. The situation was becoming impossible both for the fowl and sport when the local clubs, assisted and advised by WAGBI (The Wild-fowlers' Association of Great Britain and Ireland), negotiated leases on virtually all the marshes and restricted day permits for visitors to a sensible level. The Wash is still over-shot and results, other than for knowledgeable locals, are sparse, but disaster has been avoided.

On the wet side of the sea wall at Shep White's was moored the houseboat of that colourful character Kenzie Thorpe, one-time assistant to Peter Scott and now a professional wild-fowling guide. Tales about Kenzie are legion and none of them have shrunk in the telling, for, as is the way when the news media find a character, he has had much publicity. He is certainly not a man to take to tea with a maiden aunt. I remember walking back from flight one morning along the sea wall when, passing Kenzie's dwelling (at that moment technically a house for the tide was out and it sat in the creek bottom at a drunken angle), he emerged. Clive was beside me with his single-barrel 8 bore on his shoulder and we called a good morning over the creek. Kenzie, to whom we were complete strangers, stared at the 8 bore, shouted 'What's that —— gas pipe?' and retired, slamming the cabin door.

It was about that time I met Ray Issit, who must then

have been one of the most dedicated pursuers of geese in England. Ray was manager, foreman and labourer combined, of a small farm adjoining the sea wall and, I suspect, went into a form of mental hibernation between the departure of the geese each spring and their return in the autumn. Like all true wildfowlers he loved the geese but I have neither space nor inclination to explain to any non-shooting readers how a man can have a passionate love for the things he tries to kill. Certain it is that if the wildfowl of Britain were on the point of extermination the strongest efforts to save them would come from the wildfowlers—and not with the sole object of preserving their sport. Anyway Ray lived for the geese and for his large family, but in the winter the geese came first and when the moon was right he would spend night after night lying on the banks of the dykes, his boots slipping on the ice in the bottoms, waiting for the great grey birds. The association with him was slow to develop for all the Wash locals are bothered by visiting gunners who expect free advice on how to spoil the locals' sport. Clive and I won his confidence to the point where we were allowed to lay out our sleeping bags in his 'chitting shed'—a vast greenhouse for drying seed potatoes. The next year we progressed to the workshop, then the kitchen, and now, on my all too rare visits, I have my own bedroom. It is a great experience to leave the bustle of Surrey and eventually finish by the different world of Ray's fireside listening to wildfowling tales old and new. He has had little education and no opportunity to acquire material things but, like so many countrymen, once he accepts you he is kind, generous with all he has and wise in a way rarely found among his urban contemporaries. The closeness of the family would be an object lesson to many much better-off homes.

If you have never been fowling on The Wash you should go, for it is a rare experience. You are most unlikely to shoot anything but it is well worth a considerable journey to experience the unique atmosphere of the place. The Wash is sad and grey and goes on and on with absolute flatness, apparently for ever. By no stretch of the imagination is it beautiful but it is bare and primitive and stirs something elemental in me and, judging by their writings, many other people as well.

The next most enthusiastic wildfowler of my acquaintance is the managing director of a nationally known company, who five days a week drives, or is driven, to his office in a Jaguar. On the sixth I often pick him up and we drive to an East Coast estuary where he has a remarkable knack of attracting a heavy coating of mud in no time at all. He is the dirtiest wildfowler I know. Charlie Swan, well known in WAGBI as the man who supplies the duck rings, once told him, 'You bring more mud off the marsh on your gun than I do on my boots.' Which is true, but he also brings off a lot of duck in the course of each season.

Our American friends, of course, have a craze to own ever bigger and more powerful guns—in fact they seem to spend more time over their weapons than they do actually shooting things. It is interesting to speculate on their desire for more power. The stock explanation is that Americans must always have the biggest but like most sweeping answers, it is incomplete. I suspect that in a troubled society the sense of security given by owning a weapon also plays a part and, *ipso facto*, the more powerful the weapon the greater the security.

The biggest gun I ever handled was the double-barrelled 4 bore bequeathed to WAGBI by Beris Harcourt Wood. By arrangement I collected it on one of my Norfolk visits, to pass it on eventually to the Association's headquarters. Undeniably it was impressive, solidly built (I cannot write 'made') and huge. But the weight! No normal man could enjoy carrying and firing it, even ignoring the recoil. Once 12 bore magnums firing 2 oz. of shot became available the big bores reached their twilight.

Logically every shooting-man should use a 12 bore and, except on rare occasions, fire Number 6 shot from it. Fortunately shooting-men are not all logical and there exists in this country a strong small-bore cult, possibly for the converse reasons that promote big bores in America. We British tend, as I have mentioned, to have a guilt complex over guns and perhaps we feel a small one is not as sinful as a large. Certainly, most people who have no experience of them underestimate the killing power of smaller bores. I once bought my wife a 20 bore and, flighting pigeons at dusk near Newmarket, I lent it to a keeper friend. He was so impressed that he traded in his 12 bore for a 20 bore and for years after accomplished prodigious deeds with the little gun including a regular annual bag of several foxes. A constant programme of either pregnancy or weaning prevented my wife using the 20 bore and by the time she retired from producing children the eldest boy was firmly in possession. He and I have shot together for five years now and I have seen enough to satisfy me that if age obliges me to use a 20 bore I will do so with confidence. This said, there is no point in a fit, normal man limiting his range and pattern by using a gun smaller than a 12.

Much can be told of a man by the way he handles his gun—not simply on safety grounds, which is a strong guide, but the way he *treats* a gun. Some men seem to have no regard for it at all, treating it as so much replaceable wood and metal. It is the same men who never show respect to their quarry and will kill a pheasant by holding its head and whirling the body round in a circle, talking the while to a companion. I recall a wealthy builder who would quickly ruin the fore-end of a gun by using it to hold down barbed-wire fences while he crossed.

The attitude of men towards gun safety is interesting, but I have been often surprised to find that, contrary to reason, the most intelligent men are not necessarily the safest. In particular I have in mind a surgeon who always shot as if he was looking for business. Then there was the managing director of a large company who asked if he could bring his son to shoot on a grouse moor where I was syndicate captain. Knowing the boy was fifteen I asked if he was experienced. 'Oh, yes,' came the amazing reply from an experienced shot, 'he's shot in his school rifle team.' I pointed out that this was no experience for a grouse moor and suggested he should have some coaching at clays. Father thought it was not necessary. 'Very well,' I said, 'I'll arrange the draw so he occupies the butt on your right throughout the day.' Two days later came a note to say the boy was having coaching but I still fixed the draw. The amazing thing about unsafe shots is that they either deny having sinned or refuse to accept that what they do is dangerous. I have faced a man with a couple from the next butt who had just been splattered with his shot and the wife's face saved by the fact that her husband wore a leather coat, only to find the culprit indignant at the suggestion he was dangerous. A month later he nearly shot me in a field of Surrey stubble.

With some men the desire to shoot fades with time. Oliver Kite, that famous and warm-hearted fisherman and TV broadcaster, was once a keen shot. Before his tragically early death deprived us of one of the most human and sensible of writers on fishing and the countryside, I spent the occasional day by the water with him and several times questioned him on the point. He was, for him, strangely vague, saying simply that the desire had left him.

With others the thrill of the sport persists all their lives. I had an excellent, and touching, instance of this in the season before I wrote these words. For many years the father of a close friend had run an excellent pheasant shoot in north Norfolk and they had kindly invited me once or twice each season. In the summer the father, by then growing old, was taken ill, had a major operation and was eventually told it was unlikely he would live until Christmas. His response was to fix the dates for the season's shooting and announce that he was going to enjoy every day's sport he could and that, if he died before 1st February, nothing was to be cancelled. I was invited for a date in mid December and, when I arrived the preceding evening, saw him for the first time since his illness. Even if I hadn't known the truth, it would still have been obvious he was a dying man, hollowed cheeked and shrunken. The next day they took him from stand to stand in a Land-Rover and sat him on his shooting stick. He sat slumped and lifeless but when a pheasant flew for him I noted how he stood and threw up his gun with all the old vigour. They put him to bed when the shoot ended and before I left for Surrey I sat beside him and chatted. I said I would see him at the cock shoot in January and he said he was looking forward to it but we both knew better. When I left he looked straight at me and said he had had a good life and I shook his hand and said good-bye. The last thing he said to me was, 'You know I didn't shoot very well today.' He died four days before the cock shoot.

There was a sequel which involved one of his guns. The following summer his son, who is not a shooting man, asked if I was interested in his wildfowling gun. It turned out to be a weapon of great character, a 12 bore magnum by Lincoln Jefferies, chambered for 3¼-in. cartridges and proofed for 2 oz. shot. A non-ejector, with a pistol grip, it was entirely functional, and had the attraction of things that are simple and straightforward. To add to its character the engraving was of wildfowl and to a high standard. Its appearance coincided with a growing conviction in my mind that the use of light, standard guns for wildfowling had gone too far and I bought it gratefully. Through the early autumn the grouse took priority but in late October I took it to the Medway for a tide flight. It was a poor day for wildfowling with bright sun and no wind. I got the decoys arranged on the mud and the hide built at low water and, as the tide made and the decoys floated off, the fowl began to move. Considering the conditions there were a lot about but, of course, they were high. I missed the first two wigeon completely and decided the weight of the gun was upsetting my timing and more lead was required. A party of teal came down the creek and, as they crossed to my right, I took a right and left. Minutes later I killed a wigeon first barrel and shortly after missed another with the first and killed it with the second. The more I shot the more my confidence in, and liking for, the gun grew and by the time the tide was falling I had eight wigeon and six teal in the hide. I lay there, looking out across the rapidly emerging mud at the decoys, feeling the wood and metal of the gun, and it crossed my mind that if the dead observe the living the old man would be well content.

CHAPTER TWO

TROUT AND THE CONSTANT MAGIC

I would be happy to think that all politicians, and other men who help to shape our lives, were trout fishermen. In order to explain this sentiment, perhaps I should distinguish between the two philosophies of fishing for trout and for salmon. To fish for salmon is an end unto itself and the first success marks a true angler, whether male or female, for life. I dare to speak for women on the strength of a charming old book, unearthed in a most disorderly bookshop in Guildford, published in 1890 under the title of *Sporting Sketches* and with the nom de plume of Diane Chasseresse apparently hiding a woman of rank and wealth. Obviously she was one of the pioneers of women's lib. for the chapter on dress contains the advice, 'Stays are useful for warmth and support, but the lace should be left unfastened at the back to give free play to the lungs when taking violent exercise.' Useful as this advice may be, it is her views on salmon which concern us, and on taking her first fish of 20 lb. she wrote, 'It was a proud moment for me; one of those moments in which one feels there is nothing left to live for.' And there you have salmon fishing—a sport of great drama in which you are lifted to the pinnacle of joy or dashed into the valley of gloom.

Not so the pursuit of trout. This is a gentle sport for thoughtful people, where the act of catching the fish is a small part of a much greater whole. With a few extremely rare exceptions all the trout fishermen I know are most pleasant folk: generous of advice, helpful to the young, kind to their wives or husbands (as the case may be) and, relatively, free of envy at the success of their fellows. It may be that fishing for trout makes men pleasant, but the truth, I suspect, is that being a pleasant fellow is a prerequisite for being an angler.

I find it difficult to imagine a man who delights in all that goes to make trout fishing—the fascination of the fly box, the song of the river, the rise of a steadily feeding trout, the life and the sounds along the banks—showing aggression and rank unreasonableness to the point, for example, of plunging a country or a continent into war. Hence my opening sentence that I would be happy to think that the men who shape our lives were trout fishermen.

Some are, although alone their gentle natures cannot stem violence, as witness the fact that one of the classics of trout fishing literature, *Fly Fishing*, came from the pen of Viscount Grey of Fallodon, who was the British Foreign Minister from 1905 to 1916. To me, and possibly because I too work under pressure, the outstanding impression of this book is the great pleasure he gained from leaving the tremendous pressures of his work and relaxing for a few hours by a river. Of work and fishing he wrote, 'Then there comes the longing, which is intense, to escape, and be again among the surroundings that we remember.' If you have never read this, as it were, mental crumb from the range of Grey's activities then you should hunt down a copy. Not for what it will teach you about fly fishing, which will be little, but to enjoy the philosophy of the art unfolded by a great mind and lucid pen, and to sense the almost painful desire of a man who yearned to fish but whose sense of duty required him to serve his country. The final cruel blow came when, towards the end of his life when he could reasonably expect to relax, his sight failed. It was then he wrote the wry comment, 'On days of failure an angler may be said to go through four stages of feeling. He begins with Expectation: this is presently modified to Hope: after Hope has been long deferred the angler subsides into the stage of Resignation: finally as the day draws to a close he sinks into Despair. The angler who fishes without seeing his fly or line passes more quickly through the happier to the lower stages.'

Whenever I fish unsuccessfully and find myself growing bored or resentful I think of Grey who spent his life anticipating a retirement by the river and then, on the fringe of his dream, went blind. And I give thanks that I can fish at all, and rest content.

Enough of the angler—let us consider the fish. There are few living creatures which are so beautiful in form and movement and give so much pleasure to man, both in the catching and the eating, as the trout. Most wild things are constant in size and colour—not so the trout. From a hill loch you may take near black specimens and from a burn a mile or so away sparkling silver beauties dotted with scarlet spots. Some will have bellies of pure white and others the colour of the buttercups on the bank. The angler who travels much will catch the small, but not necessarily young, trout of an acid water Scottish loch when six will barely make the pound, yet think nothing of a two-pounder from an alkaline southern chalk stream.

A trout has none of the mystery that attaches to others of its family who disappear to the sea; it is clean, true, predictable and much studied. But for all this its natural history contains many surprises.

The brown trout (*Salmo trutta* Linn.) can be traced back to fossils some one hundred million years old in the form of the primitive group the Salmoniformes. From this has sprung a wide family of fish including the sub-order Salmonoidei which includes the various species of trout and salmon. In between the brown trout, which lives and breeds exclusively in fresh water, and the salmon which only returns from the sea to the rivers to spawn, lie various species of sea trout which spend varying periods in fresh and marine waters. This gives rise to the interesting question, as yet unsolved, as to whether the trout's ancestors were marine fish which developed the habit of entering the estuaries to lay their eggs, gradually penetrating higher up the rivers and spending more time in them, or fresh-water fish which ventured further and further into the estuaries, and subsequently the sea, to enjoy the rich feeding of the marine waters.

Trout normally spawn in November and December, although local variations extend the range to the period October to February but never beyond. The time taken to hatch varies greatly with the water temperature—from 27 days at 12° Centigrade (54° F) to 148 days at 2° Centigrade (36° F). The survival rate naturally varies greatly from one location to another but everywhere it is low. Le Cren working in the U.S.A. estimated that a typical survival pattern would show 750 fry hatching from 800 eggs. Of these only 20 would survive the first year, 10 would live for 2 years, 5 for three years and at the end of the fourth year only 2 would still be alive. This high rate of mortality applies equally to stock trout 'planted' in a fishery to improve the sport. In fact the classical research done by Allen on the Horokiwi River in New Zealand suggests that stock fish are even more vulnerable. He concluded that to produce *one* extra takeable fish (assuming a takeable fish to be three years old) it was necessary to plant either 1,250 fry, 25 yearlings or 5 two-year-old fish. This, of course, merely ensures that the takeable fish is in the water and is no guarantee that an angler will catch it.

The eggs, fry and young trout suffer many forms of predation but the common belief that the eel consumes both eggs and young and is their greatest enemy is wrong. Eels certainly take many fry but surprisingly the water shrew is the main danger, eating fry, alevins and eggs. The real sin of the eel is that it competes with the trout for the same foods.

The subject of growth is one of the most fascinating aspects of the trout. Most creatures, as they grow to maturity, reach a certain size and if there is insufficient food for them to achieve their natural development they perish. Not so the trout which simply attain whatever size their food supply permits and then stop growing. The amount of food a trout requires to maintain its weight varies with the water temperature. Other factors also occur, but in general terms at

c   33

11½° Centigrade (53° F) a trout must consume 6½ per cent of its own weight each week if it is not to lose weight. This is a very simplified exposition of a very complex subject but it is easy to see how an excess of small fish in a given stretch of water can make it impossible for any to grow larger—the production of natural food is only sufficient to maintain the fish at a given size. The solution to improving the average weight of fish caught is not, as some fondly believe, to cease fishing until the fish have had time to grow, but to fish hard so that the much depleted population can share the same food supply among fewer fish.

The growth of trout is influenced not only by the food supply but the chemistry of the water. Here again we enter into a complicated and fascinating subject but, other factors being equal, growth is good in 'hard' or alkaline waters and poor in 'soft' or acid waters. Hence, the midgets usually found in the acid waters of a Scottish loch and the large, fat beauties living contentedly in the Wessex chalk streams. The common belief that every stretch of water holds a few vast cannibal trout is inaccurate, for trout only become fish eaters when they reach a certain size and the limitations of their home waters may prevent them reaching this. The size at which they develop such nasty habits varies from place to place. In Windermere it is 12 inches but trout as small as 3 ounces will eat other fish.

In spite of its late start on fellow fish the trout is essentially carnivorous and devours a vast range of aquatic animals plus a few from the land that have the misfortune to fall, fly or be blown into the water. The majority of its diet are insects, molluscs and crustaceans; the insects being divided between those that live out their life in the water and those that emerge to breed. It was the attempt to imitate the various forms of insect, and so deceive the trout into taking a hook into its mouth, that gave birth to fly fishing and thereby bestowed one of the great blessings on mankind. Waters that contain a good supply of shrimps and snails produce trout with red spots and pink flesh, caused by the pigment carotene absorbed from this food source.

The colouring of trout is further influenced by a hormone

which disperses the black pigment, melanin, into cells in the skin and darkens the body colour when the trout is on a dark background. The opposite effect, of lightening, also occurs.

The trout is a territorial animal and having established an area defends it. Naturally the largest fish take up the best positions and continue to occupy them until they are caught or otherwise die when the next largest fish take over—a fact well known to fishermen. In contrast to the salmon, which enters its 'home' estuary and eventually the stream in which it hatched entirely by an acute sense of smell, the trout appears to have a poor sense of smell. Nor is its eyesight quite so acute as unsuccessful anglers would like to believe. As the eyes are placed each side of the head it has only a limited field of view forward so the natural fear of the angler fishing downstream that the fish is looking straight at him is unfounded. The trout's best vision is directly overhead and becomes increasingly distorted as it reaches the horizon. The important factor for the angler is that if the water is rippled the trout's vision is completely disrupted.

The speed of a trout has not been finally established but it is less than we fishermen are inclined to suggest—probably in the region of 8 to 10 knots.

The trout is indigenous to Europe, North Africa and north-western Asia. Temperature limits their spread both north and south. In the extreme north they cannot survive being frozen in ice, although they can live *under* ice if there is enough oxygen in the water. In turn this depends upon whether there is heavy snow cover on the ice which prevents the light reaching the oxygen-producing plants. Southwards trout die if the temperature of the water remains long above 25° Centigrade (77° F).

As Norfolk is mainly a county of coarse fish, my contact with trout only began when I was thirteen with a family move to Derbyshire. Never was there a clearer instance of love at first sight. I did not, of course, enjoy any fishing rights but the war was on, men had sterner duties to perform, and no one took much interest in the doings of a small boy and his bicycle. Most of the moors and rivers around the part of the High Peak where I lived were owned by the previous

Duke of Devonshire, and were he alive today I would feel obliged to write him a long letter of apology. Not that all my angling was furtive. For five shillings a day paid to the local pub I could fish a delightful small limestone river which eventually entered the Dove. It bubbled its way through the high hills nearly two leg-aching hours away, including a vicious uphill stretch through a ravine where choughs nested on the rock ledges. Petrol rationing and the call of the Services kept the opposition away and it was rare to meet another fisherman. It was good fishing by almost any standards and in a not-very-happy childhood the hours spent on that river stand out. I made the mistake of returning twenty years' later. The pub had enlarged its car park and the river was packed with fishermen favouring, in the main, worms or maggots. Precious memories are often too fragile to be re-examined closely.

My home in those days was Buxton, a town living on its past glory as a spa and growing steadily seedier as its pre-war clientele gradually disappeared. The River Wye rose in the hills, flowed through the town centre and meandered down to Dovedale, meanwhile providing a home for numerous good trout. On the high ground, where the river bubbled among the rocks, and could be crossed in a single bold step, I learnt to tickle trout, letting my limp hand wash like drifting weed along the undercut of bank or rock until it brushed against the cold flank of a fish. Slowly, almost imperceptibly at first, I would brush my hand against it until I sensed a relaxation of tension. Then I stroked it steadily, gradually slipping my hand around its body until it was cupped in the palm. The end had to come in a flash for if I misplaced the point at which I tightened my hold, or was too slow to flick the fish into the bank, it was away upstream in an explosion of fright. Now I tend to share the distaste of all adult fishermen for the art of tickling, but in all truth, doesn't it take as much fieldcraft, skill and patience as rod and line? And does the trout care how it dies? Certainly it is more humane, for the end is swift.

A mile or so downstream the river broadened and flowed through the ornamental gardens in the town centre, a place of croquet and tennis lawns, rockeries, beds and borders, and elderly retired people listening to string quartets. The paths were carried across the river on small bridges with ornamental railings on which I would lean for hours watching for the long, dark shapes of the trout below. When a fish was active I would feed it with pellets of bread, flicking them upstream and watching them drift along, sinking deeper and deeper until they disappeared down a trout's throat. The next pellet would have a Number 14 hook to gut joined to a light line which, in turn, came from a small brass reel cupped in my hand. When a trout took and I struck the problems of playing it made normal angling child's play. Not only had I to replace the give of a rod by allowing the line to slip through my fingers but I was anchored to the bridge, and if anyone appeared I had to hide the reel in my pocket and pray that the line would go unnoticed and the fish remain docile. Some mighty battles were won and lost, the more so when, in time, I became known to the gardeners. Not that they could catch me, for they invariably wore boots and my legs were hardened by the hills, but it was sad to abandon a good fish and run. I earned the money for my tackle by acting as a free-lance, part-time, press photographer for the local paper, pedalling to all the newsworthy events within twenty miles and processing the results in the basement of our house. The Editress was Jewish and as the amount of fish to reach an inland town during the war was small I usually fished on a Thursday evening and sold the catch to her on the Friday at five shillings a pound.

After a couple of years of fishing I grew very rich and was able to afford an old two-stroke motor cycle which cost me £15 and greatly enlarged my fishing horizons. By helping local farmers with their hay in return for petrol coupons I was able to make week-end expeditions to North Wales with camping gear on the pillion and my greenheart fly rod across my back. Somewhere on the Shropshire plain I would stop for a loaf of bread. If I caught trout I fried them over an open fire and ate them with fried bread, and if I failed I just ate bread. To provide variety to the cooking I sometimes cut green sticks, sharpened one end, speared the trout through the mouth and along the backbone and stuck them upright around the camp fire. I still suffer a mild pang on recalling the night I left my circle of trout roasting while I returned to the river for a last cast. Returning I found the farmer's ducks had eaten the lot and supper was bread once more.

For a man who grew up on the fast rivers of the hills, still-water fishing will always be a second best.

It was my boyhood mentor Philip Smith, who appears elsewhere in this book, who taught me the much maligned art of clear-water upstream worming. Those who are critical of this method have rarely practised it themselves—they abuse it with vague thoughts of dangling large worms in muddy backwaters of swollen rivers and catching numerous trout with no skill. In fact it calls for as much, or perhaps more, skill than fishing a wet fly, for the angler is denied the advantage of false casting. It is a good technique for the rocky rivers of the hills where the current twists and boils and a fly cannot ride for a yard without dragging or being sucked under. The fisherman works slowly and very quietly upstream, with the lightest of rods and lines, flicking a small worm into the runs where it will be carried before the eyes of the trout lying in the back eddies of the rocks. In the Highlands it is not unknown to hook a salmon and great skill and patience is needed to land it on such fine tackle. I took my first ever salmon in this way; a fish of 10 lb. on a 3 lb. line which I played for two hours and twenty minutes. It was an experience as mentally exhilarating as watching one of our children born.

Upstream worming has an extra bonus in that it involves its followers in one of the most exciting, yet unsung, of the minor field sports—that of catching the worms. Known as the garden ranger by those anglers who feel too guilty to declare its name openly, the worm can be hunted by either brawn or skill. The hard way is to take a spade to the vegetable garden, but whilst productive this gives no satis-faction. The worm is better secured by stealth at night when it partly emerges from its hole and can be easily seen on a close cropped lawn. Now some angling writers talk casually of 'picking the worms off the lawn' as if the creatures just lay there in the cause of angling. Either they are using artistic licence or they enjoy a particularly docile species of worm. Mine protrude only a wary couple of inches then, at the slightest sign of danger, flick back into the hole at a speed which makes a mouse seem a layabout. Herein lies the skill and excitement. Each worm has to be stalked as a deer lying in the heather. Only the fringe of the light may touch it and the approach must be on tiptoe lest the vibrations cause the worms' equivalent of heads in the air and nostrils flaring in the wind. Edging ever nearer the pursuer must judge his plunge to a nicety or finish up with a handful of grass and worm-casts. It is a skilful business and the fishing is almost an anti-climax. As with trout, so are worms influenced by weather. Heavy rain is ideal for bringing them to the surface, not so much during the rain as after it has stopped, but even then a strong wind will put the 'rise' down.

Time has greatly widened my experience and knowledge of catching trout. I have fished with the late, and legendary, Oliver Kite and watched him pluck a wisp of wool from his jumper and use it to tie a nymph with which he subsequently took five Itchen trout. It was done casually enough but I suspect it was a minor act of showmanship performed for many of his visitors. He was a man of great and good heart.

Then I have fished much in the Hebrides, in many different lochs that, according to the weather, looked grey and dour or sparkled like a blue and purple jewel. These remote Scottish lochs offer a tremendous contrast to the artificial still-water fishing of the South where frustrated, town-bound anglers have helped to make it economically worth-while for landowners to dig large holes, flood them and stock them with rainbows. This comment is, perhaps, unreasonably disparaging for a man who has had many happy hours on artificial waters, including the famous Enton Lakes in Surrey, but for those who have fished in remote rivers and lonely lochs, man-made lakes can offer no comparison.

This, however, is a criticism of the setting not the act of fishing. The distinction came to me forcefully this last spring. In April I had spent some time on the Hebridean island of Islay, mainly to photograph the barnacle geese which winter there. On the dull days I fished Loch Gorm, surrounded by wildlife and without the sight of either men or buildings. There were whooper swans, shortly to fly north to breed; many varieties of duck; grouse and blackcock along the banks and I surprised the occasional roe deer from its day-time cover. Overshadowing all, both in numbers and sound, were the barnacle geese, constantly passing between the loch and their feeding grounds and providing a musical back-ground of the wonderful sound of wild geese on the wing. A week or so later I was fishing a still-water Surrey lake to the background clamour of aircraft from Heathrow, cars from a main road and pop music from a fairground. It all seemed a very poor second best until the sun started to set and the fish to take. Then the truth dawned that although the trimmings may vary, the sun, wind and water are the same wherever you may be and so is the excitement and pleasure of pursuing the trout. After the first few days of freedom stock fish can be just as wary and choosy as their wild brethren and, whatever those superior beings who have the time and opportunity to fish for nothing but wild trout may say, they are not easily taken.

The business of taking trout, from whatever waters in whatever surroundings, is a constant magic—a fascination known and appreciated only to those who actually experience it. I have only to watch the intense concentration and bubbling excitement with which my young sons fish to know that it will always be so.

CHAPTER THREE

ON RATS AND RATTING

At first thought it is difficult to justify a chapter on such an unpopular subject as the rat, hated, and by some, feared more than any other creature in this country. It is true that the rat is little written about but I grant it space for the twin reasons that it casts its shadow over the whole country-side and gave, and to a lesser degree still gives, much sport. It is doubtless true that every living creature has a part to play but most of us would gladly do without rats; dirty of habitat if not habits, destructive, cruel and carriers of disease, every man's hand is against them and any method of destruc-tion is considered acceptable. This fact emphasizes the illogical and sentimental attitude of most of the public to animal welfare, for if a fraction of the cruelty sometimes meted out to rats were applied to calves or broiler hens there would be a public outcry.

I have a vivid memory of a crofter, in a remote corner of Skye, telling me how to get rid of rats. The cure, he stated with assurance, was to put down a cannibal rat. Really, said I, but how did one get a cannibal rat? It was dusk at the time and we stood on a black outcrop of rock with the Atlantic heaving behind and a breeze ruffling the dead sea-weed at our feet. It was a fine setting for tales of rats. 'Why,' he said, 'you catch three rats and put them in a metal box with air holes but no food or water. After a fortnight there'll only be one left and he'll be a cannibal.'

In fact, rats do not have to be starved in order to practise cannibalism. Visiting The Wash on a wildfowling trip I stayed with a farmer friend who complained of a rat invasion in his barn which centred on a large tub of corn. I suggested we crept into the barn after dark, when he could switch on the lights and I would shoot into the tub. In the event when the lights went on a fantastic number of rats fled in every direction and I finished up shooting only one and making numerous dents in a corn auger. Being pressed for time we left the body and next morning it had been half eaten.

Much as we may dislike rats they are remarkable animals with a rare ability to spread and survive. Although we speak of them as if they were one species, the rat found almost universally throughout Britain is the brown rat (*Rattus norvegicus*), which has only comparatively recently replaced the black rat (*Rattus rattus* Linn.). The black rat was originally distributed in the Indo-Malayan region and some authorities believe was carried all round the world from the Middle Ages onwards. Others, however, maintain that much older remains have been traced in Bavaria, Austria and Hungary. Whatever the truth the black rat was certainly well established in Britain by the time the brown rat appeared early in the eighteenth century. It appears to have come from Central Asia, crossing the Volga about 1727, reaching England in 1728–9, Germany by 1750, Paris in 1753, Norway in 1762 and Spain in 1800. Weighing approximately two and a half times as much as the black rat, the brown rapidly ousted it and today the black is only found in sea ports, Lundy and the Channel Islands. The black is a better climber than the brown, living in roofs and walls, whereas the brown lives mainly on or under the ground, and being a better swimmer will tolerate a wetter environment. In the few areas where the two species overlap the brown exist at ground level and the black above.

The ability of the brown rat to colonize was not confined to Europe for it reached the Eastern United States in 1775 and moved west to reach Wyoming in 1919 and Montana by 1923. Now it can be found from the Arctic to the Antarctic, although it is reported to suffer badly from frost-bite in the Alaskan winter.

In the first chapter I mentioned my childhood years spent on the Norfolk farm and it was here that I had my first encounters with rats in days when 'Warfarin' was unknown. They were never less than plentiful and often a plague. Each winter they moved into the warmth of the farm buildings and stackyard and each spring they returned to the surrounding fields. To quote a textbook, 'The species is largely parasitic and dependent on man.' Once they were back in the hedgerows, the spaniel and I made it our business to pursue them, not casually but with dedication. Each morning, after breakfast, we departed with our sole piece of equipment, a short-handled metal coal shovel, and each evening we returned with a bundle of dead rats, dangled by their tails, as proof of our prowess. This comradeship is no doubt where I conceived my love of spaniels, for if ever human and dog worked, thought and shared triumph and failure as one, we did. The tactics were simple. We worked the hedgerows until we found a rat-hole, when the spaniel would snort to clear her nostrils, take a long sniff, then either move off or begin to dig. If she announced a resident, and she was never wrong, I would find the other holes to the system, block all but one, station the spaniel near it, and take over the digging. Eventually the rat would bolt, the spaniel would snap it up and the sniffing procedure would begin again elsewhere. Sometimes the rat, caught in a dead-end, would bolt my way, to be clonked over the head with the shovel. We were a great team, hard-working, efficient, non-union members, with no overheads and asking only to be left alone except for regular feeding. When I look back I cannot detect a lot of difference in the mental attitude between the me of thirty-five years ago with grubby knees and a bundle of rats and the me of today in plus-twos with a brace of pheasants.

Harvest-time provided rare opportunities. Slowly the binder would clank round the perimeter of the shrinking central core of yellow corn. The men, armed with rusty,

43

elderly and frequently dangerously handled guns would deal
with the big game—the rabbits and occasional hare. The dog
and I watched for our special quarry, which to me looked
enormous. A common trick of the rats was to slink out when
the binder was on the far side and creep under a sheaf of
corn. These were easily slain. Holes, in the cornfield at least,
were rare and not very deep and therefore easily dug out.
A simpler trick if a pond or stream was near was to pour
several buckets of water down in rapid succession. I recall
seven rats emerging from one hole in an unbroken line of
wet, choking creatures and creating half a minute of chaos.

With the arrival of the cold weather and the shift of the
quarry from the fields to the buildings, tactics had to change.
Nowadays any such concentration of rats is rapidly dealt
with by poison but then the trap and gun were the main
weapons. The concentrations really could be tremendous.
In the main barn was a vast open wooden tub which con-
tained bran for immediate use. This was the prime target
for the rats each night and in it my uncle would bury several
gin traps. Each morning the victims lay there but the
remainder were undeterred. One night he decided to sleep
in the old Austin car which lived in the barn, leaving the
barn light on with the intention of letting off a couple of
barrels into the tub when the rats arrived. He dozed off
and when he woke saw such numbers of rats that, he assured
me, he was too afraid to lower the window of the car to
shoot. The great evening sport, before bed, was to wander
quietly round the buildings with a spotlight taped under the
barrel of a ·410. The beam was then played along the rafters
and when a rat was illuminated the trigger was pulled. It was
an eerie and exciting game on a blustery night as the light
picked out the occasional pair of little pink eyes.

The spaniel and my uncle's lurcher were great workers
along the hedgerows at night. I have watched one by the
light of a full moon and in a heavy frost stand motionless
with its legs astride a run in a hedge, while the other has
worked the hedge until a rat scuttled along the run to be
snapped up. It was a ruthless, never ending war, pursued
with bitter hatred by countrymen who loathed rats.

44

The pigsties were roofed with corrugated iron and insulation came from a thick layer of straw sandwiched between the iron and chicken wire. This straw made a cosy winter home for the rats and was riddled with runs. Whenever there was half an hour to spare a favourite sport was to prod the straw with pitchforks until a rat was located, when it would flee through the straw making a sufficient disturbance to show its whereabouts. Pandemonium reigned with everyone trying to spear it and the tines of the thrusting forks rattled away on the tin roof like machine guns. Occasionally a shrewd thrust would settle the matter in the roof but more usually and understandably the rat would flee down a wooden upright to the ground. The turmoil would increase as pitchforks were dropped and the rat was pursued around the sties with sticks, the excitement being intensified by the presence of the pigs.

These, however, were but minor tactics. Each year saw two major onslaughts against the rats. The first was known simply as the 'rat day' and each farm had one. Like most communal agricultural activities, particularly before television, it was also something of a social occasion. About mid-morning, their essential tasks done, our neighbouring farmers would arrive with ferrets, guns and a motley collection of dogs. All but the heaviest equipment would be trundled or hauled from the buildings to reduce cover to a minimum, and then the ferrets would be put into every reachable rat-hole. For a minute or two nothing would happen and this interval was filled with ominous clickings and snappings as the guns were loaded and closed (nothing of any real power for fear of damaging the buildings—mainly garden guns with the occasional ·410).

Then the ferrets would begin to find the rats and the fun began. Cornered rats would turn on their pursuers, screaming with what I imagined to be fury but was probably fear, and fights to the death took place in dark inaccessible corners. The bumpings and bangings produced by a large rat and a good ferret were considerable, the more so when magnified by the confined spaces of combat. But most of the rats did not fight but fled—along beams, up and down the stanchions,

45

in and out of gutters and downpipes. Taken by surprise, with anything up to a dozen ferrets loose and frequently finding escape routes blocked, they showed themselves everywhere. If they once touched ground the dogs had them, and immediately they emerged elsewhere the guns roared, or so it seemed to a small boy for, in view of the calibres, popped would be a better description. Roaring or popping they did the job and the rat slaughter was prodigious. Unfortunately the ferrets did not escape unscathed. Some died fighting in places that had not seen daylight for a hundred years. Others limped out bitten, clawed and covered in blood. I remember my mother being in charge of ferret first aid and bathing them gently for, except when working, they are mostly pleasant creatures. Once treated, the lightly wounded were returned to duty in the front line and the more serious cases were returned to the straw beds in their wooden boxes to be taken home to convalesce.

When all the buildings had been dealt with, the equipment returned and the score totalled, came the tea, with everyone in great spirits as a result of successfully battling with the rat.

The second day of great slaughter was the annual threshing. On big farms this would take several days, giving the rats a chance to escape overnight, but we were small enough to finish in a day. The previous afternoon the great, earth-shaking, magnificent steam-engine would snort and belch along the lane, drawing the vast threshing machine. After much discussion and manipulation the two monsters would be positioned in the ideal relationship to each other and the stack, the operators would untie their elderly bicycles from the back of the thresher and cycle off into the winter gloom. At first light we would encircle the stack with a three foot high wall of fine wire netting pegged well down at frequent intervals. Shortly after the bicycles and their owners would return and threshing, that most filthy occupation, would begin. Clouds of dust would fill the air and, if the day were mild, mix with one's sweat. The engine would thunder away eating sack after sack of coal and hissing in satisfaction. Meanwhile the stack went down and the pile of corn-filled sacks went up. The rats in the stack, no doubt fleeing from the heavy feet of the men working above, went to the lower level but refused to leave the shelter of the stack. At last, when the height was down to a few feet they began to bolt. Some, undoubtedly, had the cunning to bury themselves into a sheaf of corn thinking that this way lay escape. In reality they went down the throat of the monster, no doubt eventually forming a small and indistinguishable part of countless loaves of bread devoured by the great British public. The majority simply slipped out of the bottom of the stack and made a run for it, only to come up against the wire fence. Once again the slaughter was immense, and this time more complete for there was no escape.

These were very productive occasions but possibly the most sporting were the 'after closing time' forays. These were days when life for the working man, and no man worked more than the small farmer, offered little entertainment. The village pub was possibly at its peak with just enough money about for limited drinking but not enough to allow a visit to Norwich, some twenty miles away. Once or twice a week my uncles would visit one of the local pubs for darts, a pint or two and a touch of colour. I sat in the old Austin with a lemonade and packet of crisps. (When, at some social function or other, I am handed a fancy plate with a collection of nuts and some crisps, my thoughts go beyond my charming hostess and recall a variety of somewhat run-down Norfolk country pubs.) At closing time we would rattle back through the lanes singing 'Shine on, shine on harvest moon' until a mile from home when complete silence would be observed. For the last four hundred yards the drive ran slightly downhill and, with the engine switched off, the car would freewheel silently (well, almost) through the gates and into the big barn.

Now the big barn had a grain loft over the top which was reached by wide wooden stairs. At one time it had been vermin proof but the rats had now found their way in. However, on these nights we helped them by leaving the trapdoors open. As the car braked to a halt we leaped out, switched on the lights, grabbed the sticks placed in readiness and rattled on the foot of the stairs. Sometimes only a half dozen or so rats would rush down but on others there would be a brown flood. Of course, many got away but the mood of the evening was such that it mattered very little. Finally we would climb the stairs, close the trapdoors and winkle out the crafty ones which had chosen to hide rather than flee.

Rats rank among the more intelligent of creatures, a fact that does nothing to improve our liking for them. Once, in the Hebrides, I took three brace of grouse to an old game larder which I suspected could be entered by rats. As a precaution I hung each grouse by tying its head to a nail in a horizontal beam, so placed that no rat could reach the body. Next morning each grouse lay on the floor, wholly or partly eaten. On the beam above hung six heads, all neatly chewed through at the neck so the bodies would fall.

It is an uncomfortable fact that whenever man drops his guard the rat is the first creature to take advantage and move in. My father has horrifying stories of the rats in the trenches of the First World War, and it is noticeable how many writers, recounting their personal experiences of that war, refer to them. The simple but logical fact that chilled me most was that the only time the front-line troops had relief from them was after an attack, for then the rats moved into no-man's-land to live on the dead.

The ability of the brown rat to survive and thrive almost everywhere is not surprising for it will eat practically any-thing—birds, other rodents, lizards, insects and spiders, garbage, seed, vegetables, fruits—I have even known rats eat the paper labels off tinned food. Much of their success at surviving is owed to their fecundity and it is interesting to observe how this varies according to the situation and other factors. For example, the number of embryos varies accord-ing to the weight of the mother and can be as few as 6 at 150 grammes (about $5\frac{1}{4}$ oz.) or as many as 11 at 500 grammes (about $17\frac{3}{4}$ oz.). Litters also vary according to conditions from 3 to 6 per year, reaching the highest in a constant environment such as a corn rick. Females become mature when 80 days old and gestation takes only 24 days, the actual number in the litter also varying. In England research showed the average young in a litter to be 7·8 whereas in Baltimore it was 9·9.

A little arithmetic based on these statistics produces frightening results but nature, as usual, provides safety valves. Research done in 1953 suggests that when a population reaches saturation point there is a high mortality of young, both in the nest and just after emergence, often as high as 99 per cent. A further limitation is the surprisingly high adult mortality rate. In one study, based on over a thousand marked rats, only 5 per cent lived for one year. Of every 100 born in early spring, 74 were still living by the late spring, 60 by the summer, 54 at the end of the summer, 27 by the beginning of autumn, 15 at the end of autumn and 5 by the winter.

As an enthusiastic photographer of wildlife I have failed for too long to gain a good photograph of a brown rat. My collection includes various shots of dead rats in traps but not a single live study. A year ago I was driving slowly along a lane on The Wash when I passed a large rat sitting on the edge of the road drinking from a puddle. I stopped and looked back and the creature ignored me. It was, I concluded, in the first stages of poisoning and was very likely to remain while I photographed it from the car with a telephoto lens. I engaged reverse gear and gently eased in the clutch. At that moment a small, muddy car came around the corner. Quick as a stoat the driver summed up the situation, slowed, peered intently through the windscreen and carefully squashed the rat with his nearside front wheel. As he passed me he waved cheerfully with an expression that said, 'There, saved you the trouble.' I looked at the brown and red blob on the road and waved back.

Indirectly rats were responsible for another amusing experience. I was staying with a farmer friend in north Norfolk who had been troubled by large numbers of rats on his sugar-beet. It was now January, the beet was away but the rats remained and we decided on a mechanized rat hunt. The night was very cold with a hoar frost and the fields were easily crossed in the old Morris Minor he used for getting around the farm. I sat on the bonnet with my feet on the

D 49

bumper, although not without some discomfort as those who know the shape and position of the maker's symbol on that particular vehicle will appreciate. My friend then drove around the headlands of his fields, headlamps blazing, while I held onto a wing mirror with one hand and a 12 bore with the other. It was certainly not an activity I would recommend for novice shots or old men, but it worked extremely well. The rats were out in the fields to feed and as we approached they would run for the hedge whereupon the driver stopped and I shot them. This required more skill from the driver than the Gun for if he stopped too slowly I had to shoot from a moving car and if too quickly I slid off the front, encountering the symbol on the way. These problems apart I had shot more than fifty rats when I suggested we stopped as, after two hours on the bonnet, I was very cold. My host agreed, but suggested we returned home by a small private lane. This we did, and the lane being rather wider than the beam of his headlamps could cover, he zigzagged his way down. Suddenly I noticed a large object lying in the grass on the verge, and starkly silhouetted against the white frost. My friend had also spotted it and drove straight towards it. At about twenty yards I realized it was a man, lying face down, and, to put it delicately, from the waist down he was very lightly clothed. My friend, from his position of lesser vantage, could not see clearly and kept going. At ten yards I realized that the man was alive and well and that, again putting it delicately, he was not alone. At that instant the truth dawned on my driver who veered off and continued home.

Twenty minutes later, with my frozen hands clutching a mug of coffee, my friend said, 'Trouble with you Surrey people is you're too soft. Complaining about being cold when you're fully clothed—look what the natives get up to.' I agreed (one always agrees with Norfolk farmers), but suggested he was overlooking the best aspect of the incident. 'Consider it', I said, 'from the couple's point of view. All is quiet when suddenly a car roars into view, zigzagging down the road with headlamps blazing, obviously looking for something and with a man sitting on the bonnet holding a shot gun. Imagine the poor chap's feelings as, with the head-lamps picking out his unprotected rear, he said to the girl, "My God—it's your father!" '

Next day, at the formal pheasant shoot, I looked at the line of beaters advancing towards me through the kale and wondered if one of them bore me a grudge for disturbing his private life.

CHAPTER FOUR

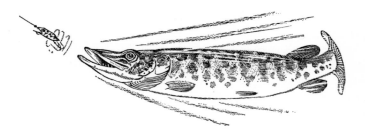

THE FASCINATING PIKE

There are not many men who come to fishing late in life—the fascination for the mysterious, half-seen things in the water and the desire to catch them is born in one and it needs little encouragement or opportunity to begin. For a boy, only just emerging from a child's world full of monsters and dragons, the pike is a fascinating creature—big, green and ferocious, with a vast mouth full of teeth, and surrounded by legend and mystery. The rare capture of a big one only serves to confirm the suspicion that every large clump of reeds or deep, slow pool conceals a long, deep-bodied piscine tiger. It is a fascination that endures throughout the fishing lives of most men and even a long succession of small jack does nothing to shake their belief that the real big 'uns are lurking malevolently in the dark places if only they can be tempted. William Senior, once Editor of *The Field*, summed it up well when he wrote, 'The pike is a most convenient fish for the exercise of imagination.'

This being so it will be no bad thing if I begin this chapter with some facts of the pike's life. They spawn in March and April and deposit their eggs on submerged vegetation, showing a preference for some forms of underwater growth but making do with whatever is available. The number of eggs laid by a given size of pike can vary widely. For example, pike of 10 lb. have been known to lay as many as 122,000 eggs or as few (perhaps the wrong word!) as 85,000. The time taken to hatch varies with the temperature of the water and experiments carried out by Swift in 1965 showed this time to vary from 26 days at 6° Centigrade (43°F) to only 5 days at 20° Centigrade (68°F).

There are many fanciful stories about the life-span of the pike, the best, or worst according to whether you believe a little exaggeration adds spice to life, claiming 267 years. The truth is less exciting for it is very rare to find a pike older than eighteen years. One naturally assumes that the biggest, oldest and fiercest pike will be males but surprisingly they are invariably females. The amount of research done on the ages of pike is limited, but the evidence is that female pike live between ten and eighteen years and males rarely more than five. Which leads us to the fascinating subject of the weight of pike. As Senior says, the pike lends itself to the exercise of imagination and nowhere does a man's mind enjoy greater freedom than on the weight of fish. (I recall the managing director of a sizeable company once solemnly assuring me that the trout he had just taken from a Scottish loch weighed 1½ lb. I gently doubted this and when it turned the kitchen scales at 10 oz. he concluded the scales were faulty.) Only last December I collected two of my sons from a day's pikeing on a Surrey lake and they showed me a large pike lying in shallow water by the lake edge which had just been caught and returned. It weighed, in a wet sack, 27 lb. and as the subsequent weight of the sack was shown to be 1½ lb. the net weight of the fish was 25½ lb. By the time the news appeared in the *Angling Times* the following week the sack had somehow been forgotten and another 27 lb. pike went into the records. At this point I must pay tribute to Fred Buller for his most excellent book *Pike* (published by Macdonald), which gathers together, and very readably too, just about everything there is to say about pike. He examines the question of weights in minute detail, starting with a list of twenty-seven pike all over 40 lb. The biggest pike ever taken on rod and line in Great Britain and Ireland weighed

53 lb. and was taken by John Garvin from Lough Conn in Ireland in 1920. One would think this event would be extremely well documented but in fact in was neither photographed nor was the body retained. The head was sent to the British Museum but when Buller inquired in 1968 they reported there was no trace of it. Subsequently he traced two enormous heads, one in the British Museum and one in the Dublin Museum and his efforts, both to determine which was the Loch Conn pike and to establish that the size of the head matched the reported weight of the fish, are absorbing and a pointer to the man's enthusiasm for all things to do with pike. The tales of longevity in pike are dealt a further blow by the fact that a reading of the opercular bone from this fish indicated an age of fourteen or possibly fifteen years.

Work done by Dr. Johnson of the Freshwater Biological Association produced evidence on the feeding habits of pike which goes far to explain how we anglers can have so many blank days when offering, with great cunning and skill, a wide range of apparently succulent baits. For centuries the pike had the reputation of a fish with a great appetite, capable of consuming twice its own weight each week. This belief was logical enough when the only evidence was the occasional capture of a pike on a live bait which might weigh half its own weight, but what our forerunners did not realize was that after a large meal a pike would not eat for a considerable time. Johnson's work has shown that a pike can maintain its weight for a year with a food intake of its own weight plus about 40 per cent. In other words, a 10 lb. pike can manage on 14 lb. of food in a year, which means that it could survive happily on five 3 lb. fish. At this rate it would only feed, on average, every ten weeks which puts our chance in a rather dismal perspective. As pike grow they must, normally, feed at a greater rate than their weight plus 40 per cent and additionally their average catch will be less than 3 lb., but the statistics are useful in that they suggest pike are very irregular feeders, even ignoring the question of water conditions.

My pikeing career began in Norfolk, the Broads of which county are famous for good fish, even though nowadays they suffer tremendous pollution from heavy boat traffic in the holiday season. In spite of the potential of my surroundings my tender years, lack of equipment and the limited range of an old bicycle, restricted my catch to the occasional small jack. My fishing horizons really opened when, at the age of fourteen, I met a Doctor of Science by the name of Philip Smith. He was old, very old, thirty-five or possibly even thirty-six, but he knew all about fishing and shooting and, having the patience of a saint, was prepared to let me question him, hour by hour. By then I lived in Derbyshire and he taught me many things about the hills and the birds, animals and fish that lived in these harsh surroundings.

It was he who gave me my first proper day at the pike and I will never forget it. For some years he had cultivated the acquaintance of a Derbyshire gamekeeper, fertilizing the relationship with regular pound notes, and the resulting harvest was the sole right to fish a small lake used by the estate as a duck-flight pond. Early on the big day, and tense with excitement for I had not developed the adult practice of refusing to expect success in order to frustrate disappointment, I cycled eighteen hilly miles to the rendezvous to arrive with the first flurry of snow, for it was January and bitterly cold. The details do not matter but in this remote spot, in the grey half-light of falling snow steadily obliterating the land, we caught a lot of pike. The lake was partly frozen over and as the day progressed we fished through an ever smaller hole. The pike had to be killed for the sake of the ducklings that would be born that coming spring, and their blood was vivid against the snow. At dusk we went our separate ways and it was a weary journey back, mainly uphill, with the tyres crunching through several inches of snow. The roads were utterly deserted and it was one of the two occasions in my life when I felt I could not go on.

Having proved my enthusiasm Philip let me have the use of one of his heavy pike rods, a fine instrument for casting large baits, built of greenheart with a tip of whalebone and more than a century old. With floats made of ping-pong balls, 25 lb. line, an old wooden Nottingham reel lovingly oiled and polished, some large trebles and a wire trace, I felt equipped

55

to tackle any pike. No doubt I was, but this leads me to a defence of the pike as a fighter, for it has a poor reputation in this respect. If one compares them with game fish it is true to say that a sea trout explodes whereas a pike simply stomps about, but the comparison is exaggerated by the difference in fishing techniques. If you hooked a 10 lb. salmon (which weight would not be a bad pike) by persuading it to take a 1 lb. herring, decorated with several large trebles, into its throat, and then played it on a heavy rod capable of slinging such a bait into the water you might not be impressed by the fighting capacity of a salmon. Conversely I have caught a pike on a salmon fly and it was some little time before I realized I was not into a salmon.

All my pike fishing has been done in winter, a season which feels right for the pursuit of such a fierce predator. In the gentle days of summer, when all is warm and plentiful, it feels proper to pursue the trout with the subtle delicacies of the fly rod or, on a sterner plane, to fish for the salmon come home to spawn, but when the hard weather comes I have the urge to seek the pike again. With absolutely no scientific foundation I convince myself that a touch of frost sharpens their appetite and so pike fishing has always meant many clothes, mittens and flasks of steaming soup.

When at the age of sixteen I advanced from a bike to an elderly 1928 B.S.A. motor cycle with narrow-section tyres and a flat tank, the fishing world was my oyster and the meres of Shropshire came within reach of my Derbyshire home. It was all I could do to afford the usual charge of five shillings a day so I slept rough in the hay loft of an old farmer with the solid name of John Brown, who had never been further from his home than Oswestry, fifteen miles distant. He sometimes referred to the steep hill that lay on my route home, but Shropshire being flat it was little more to me than a pimple. I think he suspected me of exaggerating when I spoke of the ups and downs of the High Peak area of Derbyshire. They were happy hours floating along the reed beds of the meres seeking pike with a fixed spool reel and spinning slowly with a spoon cut from sheet brass and beaten slowly to shape with a round-head hammer. But looking back, the sharpest memories are of hunting John Brown's hay loft for hens' nests and frying the eggs over an open fire while a cold dawn crept across the sky and I tingled with anticipation at both the food and the sport to come. I seemed always to be hungry in those days.

At eighteen the Army claimed me and by degrees I lost touch with Philip Smith. A quarter of a century later he saw an article of mine in *The Field* and wrote through the Editor, to renew contact. He had retired to a delightful period thatched cottage in Dorset and close to that most excellent pike river, the Stour, where he and his Irish wife (the most dedicated fisherwoman I ever met) take great toll of the local fish. When the twin commitments of business and school permit, I drive down with my boys, who have inherited at least an equal fascination for fishing, and we fish as a team. No doubt I am over-sentimental but I find it rather moving to watch Philip fishing alongside my boys, advising, teaching, encouraging and consoling, while they use rods he made for me thirty years ago.

The pike seems to be gaining favour as a quarry among coarse fishermen. This is excellent as for too long the species has been regarded as vermin to be eliminated from those waters where other fish are the prime quarry. This policy has always seemed a mistake to me for pike do not take the food of other fish—they take the fish. This must be beneficial where the ambition is to produce fish of a good size for, as I explained in the chapter on trout, a particular stretch of water can only maintain a certain weight of fish. This is not to say that the food supply is directly proportional to the size of the water—many factors affect the supply and some waters are far richer, size for size, than others. However, rich or poor in food, each stretch of water has the ability to maintain a particular weight of fish and no more. Taking a simple example, if a given stretch of water produces enough food to sustain fish totalling one hundred pounds in weight, these can be 25 four-pounders, 100 one-pounders or 200 half-pounders. This is greatly simplified but illustrates the fact that the only way, short of artificially manuring the water which practice is now evolving in America, of getting larger fish is to reduce the numbers. This the pike do, and in particular they eliminate the sick and old fish, thereby ensuring a healthy stock. A good illustration of the dangers of the argument that the elimination of predators is good for stocks is found in the campaign which has been waged for many years against otters on salmon rivers. The evidence now suggests that the prime target of the otters is eels which, by taking salmon fry, do more harm to the salmon than do the otters.

There have been so many excellent books written on the ways of catching pike that I should feel some diffidence at putting forward my views. But I am unrepentant, for no fisherman worth his salt has any doubts about his ability to dispense wisdom to his fellow anglers.

My purpose here is concerned more with weighing the different methods one against the other than with the details of the methods themselves. It is immediately important to recognize that there is a fundamental difference in the feeding habits of pike which sets them apart from other fish, for whereas most fish feed frequently on morsels, the pike, whenever possible, feed infrequently on large meals. Remembering this specific fact we can now reflect in more general terms that for any fish to take, two conditions must be satisfied—firstly it must be hungry and secondly conditions must be right. Just what mysterious combination of air and water temperatures, atmospheric pressure, rain, sun, moon and stars produce the right conditions for pike to take, I do not know. Nor, apparently, does Fred Buller, or if he does he does not reveal them in *Pike*. Reg Righyni in his book *Salmon Taking Times* (Macdonald) advances, with impressive logic and conviction, the theory that salmon go on and off as a result of the oxygen content of the water and while the behaviour of pike may have nothing to do with oxygen, Righyni shows that there can be sound scientific reasons for the apparently irrational behaviour of fish. Certainly there is no question but that pike share the fickle behaviour patterns of other fish, for there is no other logical explanation for the contrasting periods of success and failure when one fishes the same water in the same way.

However, I submit that the pike is even more fickle than other fish which, eating only small meals, at least become hungry again quite quickly and resume feeding once conditions suit them. Not so the pike, for when conditions are right only those which are hungry feed and those which still have a sizeable fish in their stomachs lie dormant. The art of catching pike therefore is to find one that is hungry and it seems logical that this is better accomplished by covering a large area of water by spinning than a small area with stationary live or dead baiting.

If this is accepted the next question is whether to spin with dead baits or artificial lures. There are three convincing reasons in favour of dead baits. One is smell. The capacity of fish to smell varies but is usually good and in some cases amazing. A good example is the details I gave earlier of the ability of a salmon to identify its own birth stream among the great waters of a tidal estuary. The portion of a pike's brain dealing with smell is not as large as a salmon's but it is still large enough to suggest this sense plays a considerable part in its behaviour. The practice of ledgering a dead herring for pike owes much of its rise to favour to the belief, by now well substantiated by experience, that the smell attracts pike. On these grounds it is reasonable to argue that a spun dead bait is rather more attractive than an artificial, particularly if the stomach is nicked slightly.

To illustrate properly the other two advantages of spun dead baits I must first submit a theory of three stages of a pike's attitude to food. In the first stage the pike has fed well and recently, is utterly disinterested in food, and would not move if the bait banged its nose. In the third stage the fish is very hungry and will take almost any bait however badly presented. (As I frequently point out to my fishing friends this condition must exist for how else can their occasional successes be explained?) The second stage is the one which interests us. In this the pike has fed recently but not too well, or well but not too recently, or any variation of quantity and time which means it is just about ready to eat again but is not over-anxious. This is a pike which is not going to swim over-far or over-fast for a bait; it is certainly not going to chase a fit fish (if indeed pike ever seriously chase fit fish rather than ambushing them) and it is likely to inspect the bait at its leisure. (Only last February I had a pike in the Stour follow my dead bait until, unable to retrieve further, I let it lie on the river bed while the fish literally pushed the bait with its snout.)

Given the truth of this argument, and it is so logical that it is difficult to doubt it, it follows that the best bait must be one which is as realistic as possible and spun very slowly—in other words, a dead bait. Further, a dead bait properly mounted, can be made to wobble like a sick fish which must have obvious attractions for a fussy pike. The outstanding feature of a dead bait against any other is that the more a fish inspects it the more realistic and attractive it must appear.

Which leads us to the third advantage, which is that a pike seizing a metal, plastic or wooden lure must immediately realize its mistake and attempt to eject it. A pike sinking its teeth into a dead bait, a genuine fish, will have no suspicions and its sole objective will be to hold tight.

The case for dead baits is so overwhelming that it is surprising that the number of spinners and lures sold must far exceed the number of dead-bait tackles. The explanation is no doubt that the inexperienced find them the obvious and easy answer and the experienced dislike using dead baits, to a lesser extent because they are messy and to a larger extent because they quickly tear off the tackle and have to be replaced. This latter problem has troubled dead-bait fishers from the time of Izaak Walton, but there is an excellent solution which I detail in Chapter 6 on tackle.

The use of dead baits also helps to solve the problem, which occupies the angling press at intervals, of whether to strike pike quickly or slowly. Given a dead bait the problem disappears for a pike is highly unlikely to eject it. As an instance, I was fishing the Stour a couple of winters ago and my companion and I took our lunch by a mill pool. He cast his sprat dead bait in and let it lie on the bottom for nearly an hour before returning to discover he had hooked a six-pounder. The condition of the dead bait showed the pike had been chewing it as a dog would chew a bone, and far from being worried by the dead bait mount, it had bent it badly.

Obviously when using a bait made of artificial material the strike must be rapid but with dead or live baits I favour giving the pike plenty of line and plenty of time.

Having argued that the best results come from covering the maximum area of water by spinning. I must concede that fishing stationary dead baits on the bottom is a very well proven and successful technique. Buller is a strong advocate of the method, arguing that pike would rather pick dead fish off the bottom than chase live ones. He further suggests that as dead fish smell more than live fish when out of water it is likely that they do the same in the water and the smell attracts the pike. This is hardly scientific reasoning but appears to be confirmed in practice as herrings, those most odoriferous of fish, are a very popular bait. Carrying the reasoning to extremes suggests it would be a good technique to cast the bait as far as possible and then retrieve it partway before allowing it to sink. This should distribute the scent over a much wider area.

Live baiting has never appealed to me, solely because I find it difficult to look the little fellows in the eye as I prick them onto a large hook and sling them out into a lake in the hope that they will be found, pursued and devoured by their natural enemy. It is illogical to be concerned about this and then to use worms which suffer the same fate plus slow drowning. But then a worm has no eyes or the elementary beginnings of arms and legs sticking out from its body to assist movement—it is so far removed from us in form that we care nothing about it.

It would be a pity to devote some pages to the business of catching pike and then say nothing about the art of cooking them. By now one would have thought the world should have reached a decision on the tableworthiness or otherwise of pike. It is far from scarce, much fished for and of such a size as to be worth some bother in the kitchen. The consensus of opinion on its culinary value should be complete. It is not. Many writers deal briefly and critically with the subject, concluding with the much used description that it tastes like cotton wool stuffed with needles. The suspicion lingers that they know little about the flesh of pike but are attracted by the phrase.

Izaak Walton, very properly, was the first man to advise on cooking pike, and started by ruling that it *must* be more than half a yard and should be bigger. You should, he wrote in *The Compleat Angler*, 'First open your pike at the gills, and if need be, cut also a slit towards the belly; out of these take his guts and keep his liver, which you are to shred very small with thyme, sweet marjoram and a little winter-savory; to these put some pickled oysters, and some anchovies, two or three, both these last whole (for the anchovies will melt and the oysters should not).' Walton continues at length, in the manner of his fishing classic, throwing in a pound of sweet butter and blades of mace, stuffing the pike with this mixture, sewing up the belly and roasting the pike leisurely, the while basting it with a mixture of claret wine, anchovies and butter. He finishes the dish with the sauce of flattery. 'This dish of meat is too good for any but anglers, or very honest men, and I trust you will prove both and therefore I have trusted you with this secret.'

After this adulation of the pike's flesh it comes as a shock to see where the *Penguin Book of French Country Cooking* puts the priorities. Seven lines only are allocated to how to boil a pike. No frills at all—just boiling. The next half-page is then devoted to making the sauce, the *beurre blanc*, with such grand comments as, 'in Touraine they naturally use the wine of Vouvray, but any light wine of Anjou would do, or even a Pouilly.'

Mrs. Beeton, without whose views no cookery comment would be complete, demonstrated the importance in which the pike was then held by listing the great variety of methods of cooking. They included baking, boiling, stewing, crimping, frying and filleting Italian style. And half a century later an anonymous clergyman in *Super Flumina*, a delightful contribution to the literature of angling, wrote, 'I buy the flesh at a shilling a pound, as it might be a salmon, but yet how cheap it is, for health and joy are given in it.' Fred Buller, in *the* book, has no time for fancy treatment, recommending boning pike carefully and making pike fishcakes. His own personal eccentricity comes at the eating stage when he recommends eating five (fishcakes not pike) then retiring to an armchair with a good cigar.

Personally I would commend the advice of the wife of my good friend Philip Smith. She is Irish and has cooked hundreds of pike, and who could dispute such a combination of authority. Take a 4 to 7 lb. pike, scale it and clean it. Stuff it with sausage-meat, herbs and knobs of butter. Cover it in fat rashers, wrap it in foil and bake it not too fast. To avoid the bones, when carving use the belly fillets. When cold the remainder can be deboned and used for fishcakes à la Buller.

The pike cannot complain of inattention in this book. We have respected him, studied him, both in natural history and in his pursuit, and finally devoured him.

CHAPTER FIVE

IN PRAISE OF PIGEONS

If I write that, taking the country as a whole and all the shooting-men in it, the pigeon gives more sport than any other quarry, then few will dispute with me.

Pheasants are renowned for their speed, grouse will swerve, duck flare and snipe jink. The pigeon has all these tricks and more besides. It reproduces in millions without the benefit of a close season; it can be killed without the need to purchase a game licence; good shooting can sometimes be had for the asking; if winged it does not race off for great distances; and when dead it has the grace to pluck easily. The pigeon is indeed a godsend to the sportsman.

Furthermore, it offers variety. You can devote a full day to it, carefully planning your campaign, carrying out a reconnaissance the previous day, and setting your decoys with infinite care. Or you can add the final spice to a day in pursuit of some other quarry by an exhilarating hour flighting pigeons into roost. And many a dull day in pursuit of some other quarry has been enlivened for me by the sudden development of a pigeon flight line, whereupon all else has been forgotten as I ambush the grey stream.

To write simply of pigeons will seem rather vague to those with a natural history training for there are more than three

64

A cold dawn and low tide on The Wash. Ray Issit waits by a main channel
in the hope of late moving fowl

2. Low tide and a successful flight. Charlie Swan, one of WAGBI's stalwarts, leaves the marsh

3. Uncle Arthur well content with a brace of Norfolk woodcock

4. The author's wife with a brace of brownies from a hill loch on the Isle of Skye

5. The late Oliver Kite takes a brown trout from the Avon

6. The author, caught in a moment of concentration, fishing a wet fly for trou
    in the Hebrides

7. A fine 3lb. rainbow trout comes to the net

Philip Smith, the author's boyhood mentor, and a dedicated fisher for pike

9.   When the rivers of the Hebrides run in spate trout fishing is forgotten. Th author by a Skye river with a brace of salmon

0.   Philip Smith gaffing a good pike from the Dorset Stour

1.   The dead bait mount described in Chapter 6 proves its worth

13.   The light fades and a Cumberland grouse moor keeper descends the hill with his dogs and a sack of grouse

14. The wood pigeon—sharp-eyed, alert, yet not so shot-resistant as some would believe

5.   A Hampshire keeper and his dogs at a January cock shoot

16. A large brown rat taken in a keeper's tunnel trap

17. The threshing machine is now a rare sight but once its arrival preceded a great slaughter of rats

8. June in the rearing field and two Cambridgeshire keepers take a breather

9. The Norfolk farmer and his spaniel

20. Springer in the snow

1. Labradors are dignified beasts and do not take kindly to being laughed at

2. 'Let's pack up—flight's over now'

hundred species of pigeons in the world (there is no difference between pigeons and doves) and five in Great Britain. But to the sportsman there is really only one species of pigeon— the wood pigeon (*Columba palumbus*). In recent years the pigeon has been the subject of one of the fascinating battles of opinion which occasionally arise between the earthy commonsense of the countryman and the carefully researched conclusions of the scientist, and this particular dispute was fought with greater keenness than usual as it hit the countrymen's pockets. The peaceful setting, soon to be shattered, that existed in the early 'fifties, saw a countryside carrying a very high pigeon population. In general terms the more intensively the land was farmed the greater the pigeon population and the development of crop rotation where cereals were followed by clover leys provided ideal feeding conditions. In an effort to reduce the crop damage done by this grey multitude the Ministry of Agriculture in 1954 introduced a cartridge subsidy scheme whereby genuine and competent pigeon shots had half the cost of their cartridges refunded. The only evidence required was the receipt for the cartridges purchased and a statement of the number of pigeons shot. The shooting community, particularly the impecunious members, entered into the scheme with the same ecstatic enthusiasm as the working classes experienced their first holiday with pay, and for much the same reason. Of course, no shooting man would have been so dishonest as to claim for cartridges fired at quarries other than pigeons, but a careful analysis of where the subsidy cartridges were discharged would have produced some surprising information about pigeons; for example, an amazingly high number appear to have been sighted over coastal saltings, and high concentrations occurred in February over the fields where hare shoots were taking place.

It was an idyllic situation that might have endured for ever had not the Ministry of Agriculture, far from being grateful to the sportsmen, instituted a research programme to discover more about the pigeon and its control. Several scientists were involved but the man who eventually emerged as the villain was R. K. Murton, who subsequently

E 65

wrote a book entitled *The Wood Pigeon* (Collins), which does for pigeons what Buller does for pike, but more scientifically. Their conclusions covered many pages but the essential message could be given in a few words—shooting pigeons did nothing to control their numbers, for the birds shot would only have died sooner or later of starvation. The shooting world was so affronted as to lose its dignity and behave like a group of Members of Parliament. Uproar prevailed. A pigeon shot is a pigeon dead, they said, and don't tell us this isn't a good thing for agriculture. The Ministry of Agriculture, who unlike most of the critics, had taken the trouble to read and consider the report, were not impressed, and in two stages the cartridge subsidy was removed, finally disappearing in 1969.

The reasoning behind this conclusion justifies more detailed examination, for it shows with stark clarity how the numbers of all wild creatures are utterly dependent upon the supplies of available food. At this stage I must make it clear that most of the data I quote in this chapter has been gleaned from the pages of Murton's book. It is a fine example of how the combination of a trained scientific brain and meticulous and lengthy observation will produce results which will often contradict the long-held, but shallow and inaccurate, beliefs of the countryman. For the wood pigeon the gap between life and death from starvation is so narrow that in midwinter it must spend 95 per cent of the daylight hours feeding. The increased daylight hours of spring are not a great help for, apart from the sudden but brief boost from the spring cereal sowings, the available food supply is still limited. In practice it is not until the grain season begins in July that the birds can satisfactorily find time to breed. Statistically this is demonstrated by the fact, from Murton's data, that 70 per cent of all young wood pigeons leave their nests in August and September, 6 per cent in July (and only 1 per cent before this month), 21 per cent in October and only 2 per cent in November. The pigeon population approximately doubles by October and this great army falls upon the stubbles to feed on the spilt grain, the old to recover their condition after breeding and the young to grow to a sufficient weight to face up to the winter. At the time of the studies most of the grain stocks were exhausted by December although, as I will show later, the position has now changed. With the grain eaten the pigeons have to subsist on clovers and weed seeds and as these have low nutritive values and the daylight hours for feeding are short, the birds are very vulnerable. There then occurs the classical situation in which nature, to ensure the survival of a species, has produced more creatures than the food of the countryside can sustain and the surplus starves. The figures are well illustrated by a study area which Murton and his colleagues observed over a six-year period. In July the population averaged 63 birds per hundred acres. In September after breeding it had risen to 154 but by February this had fallen to about 70 birds.

By now his logic should begin to emerge. If, taking the study area as an example, the ground can only sustain 70 pigeons by February it makes no difference if some of the 154 birds alive in September are shot or not—they will die anyway. Shooting would only be effective if more than half the birds could be shot and, in areas with high pigeon populations, this is virtually impossible. There is even a logical argument that shooting increases the population. Consider an individual pigeon alive in September. Left unshot it will eat merrily away until, say, February, when it dies of starvation (or disease which successfully attacks it in its weakened state—it does not matter which). In this five-month period it will have eaten a considerable quantity of food which has not enabled it to survive and is denied to other pigeons. If shot in September this five-month food supply is available. In other words, and in general terms, taking the 153 birds on a hundred acres of the study area, shooting 53 in September might leave enough food for the 100 to survive the winter whereas leaving the whole 153 to guzzle away unharmed will see only 70 alive in the spring.

It is a fascinating example of nature at work, but after this unnaturally long spell of heavy thinking we will move to lighter matters for a little.

Pigeons are shot, at least in any quantity, by either decoying, flight-line shooting or roost shooting, and as enough books have been written on these techniques (I have even added my own modest contribution), I will not elaborate but assume the reader knows at least the theories and is probably an adept practitioner as well. There is an interesting comparison to be made between pigeon decoying and coarse fishing. Both are static sports which, I suspect, appeal to men of similar temperaments—slow, thoughtful, patient men who like to work out the problems and watch their solutions succeed or fail. Most other forms of shooting are more mobile and may be compared, both in technique and the participants, to game fishing. Our coarse fishermen and pigeon decoyers, however, both select their site with great care and due regard to, in the one case, the current, and in the other, the wind. Concealment, patience and stillness are important to both, and both hunters have to lure their quarry, the one with ground bait and the other with decoys.

Both are supposed to be capable of near miracles but, judging by the success with which some coarse fishermen consistently win big money prizes, while this may be true of the fishermen I have my reservations about pigeon decoyers. I am not particularly modest about my own skill with the pigeons but I would never start a decoying day with full confidence. Pigeons are too like wildfowl—it is all very well to calculate what they should do but very often, for no explicable reason, they simply do not do it. On several occasions I have decoyed with acknowledged pigeon experts but they are equally unable to produce sport to order. Certainly they get their sums right more often than most people—that is why they are considered experts—but the point I make is that they are far from infallible.

Another pigeon point upon which much nonsense is talked is the ability of pigeons' feathers to resist shot and the consequent need to shoot them with a magnum gun. This is, I suspect, a fallacy originally fostered by the gun makers in the days when their customers were, in the main, wealthy men and the only limitation to the number of guns they could sell them was the variety of guns they could convince them they needed. Having easily preached the need for special guns for wildfowling it was a simple step to 'pigeon guns' to conquer those tricky feathers. In practice, I am absolutely sure the feathers of a pigeon have no more ability to turn shot than the feathers of any other bird and probably less. The legend owes its longevity to three factors. The first is the willingness of sportsmen to accept any explanation for the failure of the pigeon to fall other than the correct one that they missed it. The second is that the pigeon is a difficult and small target and therefore easily missed. The last is that it has loose feathers and a single pellet or so can pluck out an impressive display without actually entering the body. Off will go a startled pigeon while the sportsman looks at a snowstorm of feathers and comments that these pigeons can 'carry an awful lot of shot'. The fact is that a standard load of Number 6 shot, fired in the right direction, will drop a pigeon some yards further than a cock pheasant or mallard.

My own preference is for roost flighting rather than decoying for the sport is more certain and the shots more difficult. I accept that decoying calls for much greater skill to get the birds in range, but it is much more likely to provide a poor day and can then be deadly dull. The only really bad evening flights I have had at established roosts have been on really cold, frosty nights with absolutely no wind. On the worst occasions I have had literally no pigeons come to woods where on a normal night there would be hundreds roosting. I have never worked out a satisfactory reason. Granted the lack of wind will remove the need for pigeons to seek protection from it in the heart of a wood and any decent hedgerow will do to roost, but the habit of roosting in a particular wood is so strong that I cannot see why they should break it on these relatively rare occasions. These exceptional flights apart some of my most enjoyable hours with a gun have been spent killing pigeons in the gathering gloom with the bare branches swaying under a strong wind, the pigeons pouring in almost non-stop, and a spaniel or a young son gathering the slain from among the brambles and the dead, crisp leaves of the forest litter. Some birds come in slow and very high, peering suspiciously down through the branches; others scream in on the wind and whirl through 180 degrees to land confidently. Others, no doubt the old and wily, wait till it is almost dark and sneak in low, swooping up rather than down, to the trees on the edge of the wood. If you know your flighting you will anticipate them all, lurking in the thick cover while the light is strong and gradually emerging into the more open areas as the light goes and the pigeons grow more desperate and suicidal to drop in. It is only on these occasions that I get enough shots in quick succession to begin to handle the gun as it can and should be handled—not mounting it and solemnly aiming but throwing it into the shoulder and firing at the same instant, hardly being aware of the barrels but knowing just where I want to shoot and doing it subconsciously. So must the master shots of old have performed. I suspect there are a number of potentially superb shots alive today, possibly you sir, who, given five or six days driven shooting a week, with bags running into several hundreds each day, would rapidly have displayed a skill that never has the chance to flower on two pheasants, a hare and a jay in the course of a long, hard day's rough shooting.

A very useful accessory for roost flighting, and in some circumstances decoying, which I rarely see used, is the 'crow scarer' rope of bangers. If the pigeons cannot roost in the wood you occupy, or alternatively the crop you protect, they will soon settle into or on their second choice. The more that settle the more they attract others, and very soon your flight line can dry up. The judicious placing of 'bangers' before you begin will not only keep flocks from settling for long but quite often scare them to you. (At this point, as it was midnight, I stopped writing this particular chapter. Rising early next morning I drove to Sussex for what should have been a day's formal pheasant shooting. In fact, owing to a disaster with the keeper, our stock had gone, and with three of the other Guns I planned to spend the day rough shooting. After an hour or so had produced only one black, rather evil-looking old cock, sport was very dull. Suddenly we noticed a strong flight line of pigeons had developed across a water meadow. We abandoned the pheasants and spaced ourselves under a convenient hedge which cut at right angles across the flight line. For more than an hour we had excellent sport as flock after flock of pigeons crossed at varying heights and speeds. It was a grand example of the sport the pigeon gives to the shooting man.)

The pigeon must have been driven out of Britain by hunger at the time of the last Ice Age and recolonized afterwards. It is essentially a woodland bird and returns to tree cover when disturbed, to rest and to roost. The ability to produce pigeons' 'milk' for their young distinguishes the *Columbae* from all other birds, although the milk is mixed with other foods in the crop after the first few days. As the milk is of a high nutritive value the young benefit greatly, but it is produced at the expense of the adults' body substances. Apart from milk the main food of nestling pigeons is cereal grain and, as mentioned earlier, this partly explains why the main breeding season coincides with the ripening of the corn and the harvest. It is calculated that the average adult mortality rate is about 36 per cent, and that the average age attained by adults is thirty-eight months. Like most wild things the life of a wood pigeon is much less than its potential in captivity, where it would be protected from predators and hunger. It is thought that relatively few pigeons die directly from disease but the lowering of condition that disease brings ensures that sick birds are the first to die when food becomes scarce.

After this interlude we will return to the battle between those trying to destroy the pigeon and those anxious to preserve it for sport. Hardly had the shooting community recovered from the stunning loss of its cartridge subsidy when nasty rumours began to circulate of official, but secret, trials of tic beans treated with narcotic dope which, when eaten by the pigeons, stupified them until the farmers could collect the victims and kill them. Quickly the rumours were substantiated by official statements, dotted with statistics of the numbers slain by how many beans on how many acres. The sportsmen, sensing disaster, were incensed. Once more, uproar prevailed. Every logical objection, and some illogical ones, were submitted, of which the most telling was that the dope was indiscriminate and left game and other birds at the mercy of predators. The Ministry, not unaccustomed to criticism, pressed doggedly on and the shooters foresaw the pigeon following the rabbit and grey partridge into decline. Their gloom, or more correctly our, for I was one of the pessimists, was premature, for snags began to show. Pigeons, as every shooter knows, are unpredictable, and it is no fun to spend some time baiting a field with doped beans only to find the quarry has found another larder. Having laid the beans they cannot be picked up and the field must be visited regularly to collect unconscious avian bodies for some days. This is all very well for experiments but not practical for a busy farmer short of men. Rain affected the bait, experiments interfered with agricultural operations and, generally, it began to emerge that the technique was in danger of offending the basic rule of pest control—that the cost of controlling the pest must not be greater than the damage the pest does. The problems of the dopers were observed with scarcely concealed glee by the shooters and gradually less and less was heard of controlling the pigeon menace by dope. The lesson for all was that what can be done in a few places by determined men of single purpose is very different from the results obtained by a wide variety of men in contrasting surroundings. (One has only to look at the very different results of gamekeepers to see the truth of this.)

Content that the pigeon was safe, we faced up to paying the full price for our cartridges and assumed that we would live happily ever after. In fact in the July 1972 Game Fair number of *The Field* I contributed a light-hearted article which depended for its impact on the ludicrous suggestion that the wood pigeon would one day become scarce. In what was then intended as a joke, but may be seen in thirty years' time by a researcher as a remarkable forecast, I wrote of a shoot in 2001 in which the syndicate captain criticized a novice Gun for shooting at a wood pigeon out of season. Continuing I said, 'With the wood pigeon in danger of going the same way as the partridge, my view is that there should be a voluntary shooting ban until there is evidence of a real recovery. Still, the position may improve more rapidly than we think, for I hear WAGBI have got the blessing of the N.F.U. to launch their wood pigeon rearing scheme next spring.' Various friends thought it was quite funny.

Only a few months later the occasional letter begun to appear in the *Shooting Times* and *The Field* commenting that the writer was experiencing a shortage of pigeons in his area. Others soon wrote to say that, by coincidence, so were they. In no time the trickle became a torrent and it was obvious that pigeons were in short supply. This fact having been established, the correspondence turned to remedies, and in no time the joking references in my article to close seasons and shooting bans became solemn proposals. It is a strange world.

Many letters contended that the cause was over-shooting which, at first thought, was illogical for if the pigeons thrived when cartridges were subsidized they could hardly be expected to decline when they were not. In practice a new factor has arisen in the last few years with the growth of the export trade in frozen pigeons to Europe. Once it cost very little to shoot a pigeon but the carcase had little value. Now it costs more to shoot it but the value is far higher. This very day I received a circular offering me seventeen pence for each pigeon from a dealer who was willing to collect any reasonable number.

The theory of over-shooting seemed logical and the sportsmen were just preparing to kick poor WAGBI, which organization was progressing well with its scheme to organize ever more pigeon shooting for the benefit of both sportsmen and farmers, when Dr. Murton reappeared and announced that the shortage had nothing to do with shooting. As previously, his arguments were lucid and convincing. Pigeon numbers, he explained had only grown so high because agricultural practices in some areas provided enormous supplies of food. Now stubbles were being burnt sooner and better machinery permitted earlier ploughing. This denied the pigeons the grain which, at one time, both saw them through to November or December and allowed them to enter the hard weather in good condition. Additionally, much less clover was being grown. Less food sustains fewer pigeons and therefore it was starvation, not shooting, to blame. Go, he said, and shoot as hard as you like—it will make no difference.

I wonder. It takes a brave, or perhaps stupid, layman to argue with a scientist but I do not accept that it is invariably true that, as long as pigeon numbers exceed the food supply, shooting makes no difference. If a situation arose in which the shooting pressure became very high it would; for after nature had starved the large numbers of the autumn down to the level the land would feed, the sportsmen would go on reducing the breeding stock of the coming summer still further. Up to now the shooting pressure has never been high because there have been so many pigeons and so, relatively, few shooters that their bags have been insignificant. Nor has there ever been any prospect of a great increase in the numbers of men shooting, but the same effect is achieved if the pigeon population falls substantially while those shooting remain constant. (Fewer pigeons will not mean fewer shooters, partly because the price paid for a dead pigeon will increase and partly because many pigeon shooters have no alternative quarry.) Additionally bags will not fall in proportion to the pigeon population drop—it makes no difference whether a flock of three or thirty birds comes to the decoys for the gun has only two barrels. Given a marginal situation the question of when pigeons are shot also becomes important. Shooting a couple of pigeons in November that would have starved in February anyway makes no difference. Shooting the same pair in July, shortly before they rear two young, does. And it is often easier to shoot pigeons in the summer when they move individually or in small numbers, than in the winter when they flock.

The pigeon, I am quite satisfied, is in no danger of extinction today, but I fear the golden days of pigeon shooting are over, at least for the time being. I am happy to have experienced them. I have vivid memories of shooting pigeons in numerous counties, over all manner of crops and at all times of day—even, on one memorable occasion, shooting their silhouettes crossing the moon as they dropped into roost in the late dusk on a remote corner of the Hebrides.

On the days when all goes well the question of removing the bag is often a problem. Once I shot from a bale hide, on a clover ley in Cambridgeshire, built in the middle of an enormous field and over a quarter of a mile from my car. It was a wet, windy day and I was on a good flight line. The wind kept them low and practically every bird dipped over my decoys. By late afternoon I had 121 and it was a weary business getting them to the car along with the gun, unused cartridges, shooting stick, waterproofs, camera, thermos, decoys, camouflage net, and all the other oddments. Various friends have various systems for carrying, but the easiest is simply to chuck them in a sack. A good alternative is to take the string that every good countryman has in his pocket and knot them into two large bunches, by the necks, which are then slung back and front over a shoulder as a Frenchman carries onions.

Pigeons can play greater havoc with your percentage of kills to cartridges than any other quarry except driven grouse and wildfowl below the sea wall. Over decoys, when they are dropping in well and not circling suspiciously, a competent shot should average anywhere from 50 per cent to 75 per cent—possibly even better. But when they are dropping in to roost on a windy night, glimpsed as grey shadows dimly seen through a tossing sea of branches, and particularly when you forget percentages and go for every chance offered no matter how fleeting, 25 per cent can be not only reasonable but good. Some may look disdainful at this suggestion but before you speak, sir, of last week when you averaged 65 per cent and recount the run of six hits culminating in that right and left, please recall the two birds for seven shots at the start before your eye was in and the row of misses at the end when the light had gone. Accurate calculations of kills to cartridges call for absolute honesty and a fine memory. In fact the only certain way is to count the number of cartridges you start the day with and the number you take home.

Not that everyone is humbled by pigeons. One cold February I was taking part in one of the mammoth Cambridgeshire hare shoots and standing in a widely spaced line of standing Guns lining a hedge. Another hedge joined this at right angles and seemed to be the ground marker for a flight line of pigeons, for there was a steady trickle of birds along it. As the line of Guns was clearly visible to the pigeons but extended for at least a mile they decided not to detour but rose and crossed at a height I would have thought almost out of range. The Gun in the intersection of the hedges happened to be the then shooting coach for Gallyon's of Cambridge and, one after another, he tumbled those pigeons. It was a superb exhibition of practical field shooting which I have never seen bettered.

Most men would like to feel that they have achieved a permanent niche in history and this is an appropriate place to stake my claim. It does not, I readily concede, look impressive when placed alongside the deeds of the various giants of politics, armed warfare and medicine, but it is all I have and I cling to it. I am the man who invented the technique of making pigeon decoys by injecting whole, dead birds with formalin. The thought first came when I watched a shooting friend, who is also an authority on birds, lecturing on waders and illustrating his talk with various wings preserved by formalin injection. Some experiments soon showed that, provided the breast and stomach were adequately injected, whole pigeons could be preserved, and the birds allowed to dehydrate and harden, if adequately supported in realistic postures. Previously formalin had been used only for the legs and wings and the standard procedure involved the messy and lengthy operation of opening up the breast, removing the flesh, stuffing the cavities with a suitable material and sewing up. Not surprisingly this was evolved by a Surgeon Commander in the Navy, but I never met anyone who used it because of the time involved. Once I was satisfied that I had determined the best needle size, quantities, drying times and other data I wrote a detailed description which appeared in *The Field* in September 1965. Not entirely to my surprise the reaction from the shooting world was slight, particularly from manufacturers of rubber pigeon decoys. If memory serves me well the Surgeon Commander wrote to the Editor to explain that his method left the breasts in better shape but as decoys sit on their tummies rather than lying on their backs this was hardly relevant. It was, I thought, the end of the matter but I have been pleasantly surprised to see the occasional reference to decoying with preserved pigeons, which suggests that it is now standard practice for some pigeon shots. Most flattering of all, about every couple of years an article will appear in the sporting press from some chap or other describing how to preserve pigeons by injecting them with formalin. Next time you read one I would appreciate your thinking 'Ah! but I know who first thought of it.'

We draw near the end of this chapter on pigeons and you will notice I have said nothing about building hides, setting out decoys and the like. It has all been said before. But I will pass on one personal conclusion which may not so much help you to succeed on the days you go shooting pigeons as help you pick the days to shoot on which you are more likely to succeed—if you follow me. For years I kept a record of the weather conditions and the bag on the days I decoyed to see if there was any relationship. In time it became obvious that results were better on windy days, but for reasons I can only partly explain. For decoys to attract, pigeons must see them, and greater success obviously comes on the days pigeons are moving freely. Wind makes or encourages pigeon to move about and consequently improves the bag, but why it should do this I have no idea other than the thought that wind must make flying both easier and fun. Whatever the reason, if you enjoy a choice pick a windy day to decoy.

It is a slightly depressing thought, for me that is, that of those who will read this rather more will be younger than me than older. Those who fall in the more fortunate group should watch the future of the pigeon. It may one day need your protection for without it the sport of shooting would never be quite the same.

CHAPTER SIX

TACKLE TINKERING

You are either born a man who enjoys making things or you are not. Those of you who are not see no sense in spending an hour making something you can buy for a few pence. The others who, like me, delight in creating their own bits and pieces do not count time. The fact that you have so far been a buyer of things rather than a constructor does not mean the urge is not latent within you and the purpose of this chapter is to drag your talents to the surface.

I know I am not alone in this pleasure I gain in making, using and succeeding with items of equipment and the explanation no doubt lies in the very distant past for all field sports exist because of the deep fundamental instinct of men to hunt and an essential of hunting was the construction of the tools of the chase. At the beginning it was no doubt a simple business of gathering stones of the right size and weight for throwing. Gradually the hunters progressed to clubs, spears and ingenious devices such as rolling boulders over cliffs or digging pits, and eventually selecting the right timber to form bows and arrows. So the urge to make one's equipment derives from an instinct formed over many thousands of years. Yield to it for you may eventually grow like the fishermen who derive more pleasure from making tackle than actually fishing.

This same instinct is no doubt responsible for the contented feeling a man can gain from gazing at a well-filled tool rack, for tools are the instruments of creation and their use a source of natural satisfaction. Consider the pleasure derived from a penknife with a variety of gadgets—just a simple metal device but it nestles in the hand and gives forth a strange feeling of tactile pleasure and security. It is both a weapon and a tool and many years ago could have played a large part in your day-to-day survival.

Philip Smith, mentioned in the chapter on pike, is the greatest constructor, creator, fabricator, tinkerer or what you will, I have ever met or am likely to. A degree in engineering, a research job that gave him an infinite range of materials and tools, and a ceaseless stream of ideas and energy meant that his workshop was always packed with projects—and what is more they worked. There was the sea-going canoe which could be dismantled and its collapsible trailer with which he toured the west coast of Scotland. And the camera with a body made from the casing of a German incendiary bomb. Even now when I visit him at his Dorset cottage the workbench invariably has an idea or two taking shape.

For a teenager, fanatical about field sports, he was a marvellous tutor—willing to talk, explain and demonstrate for hours but ruthlessly critical of shoddy work or other failings. I have a reputation for punctuality which is partly owed to a severe dressing down he gave me one cold winter morning on top of the Snake Pass in the High Peak of Derbyshire. I had arrived late after puffing up a seven-mile hill on my bicycle laden with a box of ferrets. Why was I late? I told him of the severe icing on the roads and got the reply that only idle men fail to foresee and allow for adverse circumstances. At this time the war had been in progress two years and all sporting tackle was scarce or unobtainable. He taught me to equip myself by the use of everyday materials and some ingenuity. Game and fishing bags were sewn from canvas or even the printed material on which ladies embroider and form tablecloths. Under his direction I learnt the skills required to knit purse nets for ferreting rabbits, or to tap a thread onto a metal rod, forge it into a gaff and harden the metal. The particular gaff which emerged from this instruction has landed me many salmon and will land many more. In those wartime days all the nation's capacity for metal fabricating, in any form, was concentrated on priority needs and fishing rods were unobtainable. Under the master's guidance I designed and made a usable fixed spool reel from a block of well-seasoned hardwood, a sheet of electrical insulation board and odd discarded lumps of brass. Not only did it work and catch fish but it had the ability to reverse the spool and periodic reversing eliminated line twist.

Philip Smith makes his own rods and, as I write, hanging in the long line of rods on the wall are two of his, a fly and a light spinning rod, both in greenheart. They are more than thirty years old now but they still catch fish and give me infinitely more pleasure in the process than any shop-bought article. This feeling is intensified when I have made the equipment or at least some part of it myself. The trout I land on a fly of my own tying assumes in my eyes a beauty denied to other fish; I have no doubt that to a home loader of cartridges his pheasants are fatter and with a depth of colouring superior to those slain with factory-made cartridges. An excellent example of Philip Smith's ingenuity is his dead-bait tackle. I am convinced that one of the reasons this theoretically most effective form of fishing is used less than artificial lures is the need to replace a messy bait frequently. From the beginning of angling no one has devised a form of dead-bait tackle which preserved the bait for long spells, for the method of securing the bait to the tackle was invariably to use the hooks. As a result all the strain of casting and retrieving is concentrated on these very small areas of flesh, which quickly tear. Philip Smith's solution is a thin metal bar rounded into a 'U' at one end and with a series of holes along its length. The head of the fish is positioned into the 'U' and the body stitched to the bar with coarse wool (thick wool does not cut into the bait as thread would). With a little needle care the entire spine of the fish can be sewn along the length of the bar. The hole at the point of the 'U' takes a split ring (or a ring of brass wire taken from heavy-duty electric cable and soldered) and two similar rings, one-third of the distance from the head and at the tail respectively, take the treble hooks (see the photograph No. 11). The advantages over conventional tackle are both several and substantial, but foremost is the ability of the tackle to hold the bait securely for several hours' fishing as the strain is distributed evenly over the entire fish. On the all-too-frequent occasions when my bait has not been damaged by a fish I have gone through a full day with only one change. Next is the advantage of free-flying hooks, for both the trebles retain their full hooking power, not having any of their hooks buried in the fish. Less important advantages are the ability to vary the number of hooks, their sizes and position, easily, and the ease with which the spin of the returning bait can be varied by bending the bar. For smaller baits where a bar might be obtrusively wide, wire can be substituted for the metal strip and bent to form loops at frequent intervals.

The sole criticism that can be levelled against this tackle is that a fish can both see and feel the bar. My view is, so far as sight is concerned, that any fish so sensitive would be put off by the cluster of hooks surrounding most tackles. As to feel, I think this aspect is of no consequence for when a predatory fish chomps his jaws onto the victim he expects a mixture of flesh and bones and the bar or wire passes as the spine. Certainly it is ridiculous to damn this tackle on grounds of feel and then fish with a solid metal lure. This aspect leads me to the thought that we should strike harder when fishing dead baits than other lures. The conventional artificial lure is of some hard material and when the fish takes its teeth will not penetrate. Consequently the strike will pull the lure through the teeth and the hooks into their hold on the fish. With a dead bait the teeth of the fish penetrate and, unless the strike is hard enough to tear the flesh of the bait and bed the hooks, all the strike will do is jerk the head of the fish.

For those who have reservations over their skill as makers of oddments a modest start will build a confidence which otherwise could suffer early bruising. Take fly tying as an example. Attempting to produce a complex fly involving four different materials, three colours of silk and some tinsel, which not only looks good but will hold together for several hours' casting, is not so much an expression of self-confidence as arrogance which will surely be punished. Nor is such ambition necessary for two of the most successful flies I use are very simple. When there are no signs of fish moving it is sensible to fish well below the surface and for this I use a pheasant-tail nymph. In fact it is not a nymph but a simulation of a caddis-fly larvae case. (The larvae of the caddis- or sedge-flies form tubular cases from debris of all sorts and an examination of the stomach contents of a trout will often reveal what appear to be small sticks which, when opened, reveal larvae.) The only materials required are a cock pheasant's tail and some fine copper wire (5 amp fuse wire does very well). A proper fly tying vice is ideal but an ordinary bench vice can be used. Lay three strands of feather along the shank of the hook and allow them to project to form a short tail. Trap them in position with a couple of turns of wire. Then build up the body of the nymph with more strands of tail secured with occasional turns of wire. To produce a heavy nymph which will fish low use more wire and less feather and vice versa. Straggly pieces of feather sticking out at all angles should not be cut off but actually encouraged as they help resemble a genuine caddis case. Naturally this device must be fished very slowly.

The second fly represents a midge pupa on its way to the surface to hang in the surface film and eventually emerge as a winged insect. In theory it should be fished very slowly— twitched rather than retrieved, but occasionally I have had very good results by retrieving quickly. Take three strands from a peacock's tail feather and, in precisely the same way as with the pheasant-tail nymph, bind them to the shank of the hook to form a tail but use green wool instead of wire. Build a fairly thin body in the wool thickening towards the eye of the hook to suggest the thorax. Finally bind the whole body with peacock tail and take a few wide turns with fine wire to secure it.

I am no more immune to the temptation of trays of flies in a tackle dealer's shop than other fishermen and I have a grand collection of different flies, many of which have actually touched water. But taking the season through I catch more trout on the two flies described than on all the others put together.

Rod making was a great art to which many amateurs applied themselves for hours to produce but poor results. Now the availability of glass fibre blanks makes it possible to produce rods with ideal actions, although it is quite wrong to claim one has made the rod—the designer of the blank is the genius and we are merely adding the final touches. It is, however, well worth while building a rod from a blank, partly for the satisfaction, partly for the economy and partly for the ability to use good-quality fittings and ensure that they are well applied. A little extra care over details makes all the difference to the end result and with a piece of equipment which will serve you for years it is silly not to spend a little longer on its creation. Take, for example, the business of whipping on rod rings where a few seconds can improve the result. Start by securing one arm of the ring to the rod with Sellotape to ensure it is precisely in line with the other rings. Then draw the thread across a block of beeswax, which will make it more workable and help it to lie well on the rod. Work from the outside of the arm in towards the ring, rather than the reverse, as this avoids the gap which would otherwise occur where the thread ceases to cover the arm. (If the arm is too thick at the end file it down.) When the whipping is complete, roll a pencil across the surface until the threads have flattened and merged firmly against one another. Finally ensure that the varnish fills the small triangular gap between the arm, the rod and the thread which will otherwise take in water and retain it.

Having made or purchased decent rods it seems a pity to keep them in the inferior rod bags which economics force manufacturers of all but the most expensive rods to supply. This said, however, the production of superior bags is not so easy as might at first appear. Design is no problem at all, with the one proviso that you keep the individual compartments reasonably wide, for wet rod sections pushed into rather tight divisions in a wet rod bag tend to stick. Nor is the selection of a suitable material difficult provided you realize that, contrary to the need of most equipment containers, it must not be waterproof. Inevitably the rod will often be wet and the material of the rod bag must be capable of 'breathing'. The real difficulty lies in the fact that sewing a rod bag is a laborious business by hand but the work of a few minutes with a sewing machine. This may be a formidable obstacle to some but if you can overcome it do ensure that you make the best of your advantage by using really good material; so little is needed that the extra cost is of no consequence. Nor must you be bound by the sober colours of convention. I recently made a bag for a salmon fly rod of, appropriately enough, a bright Hebridean tweed, purchased direct from the crofter who wove it.

A particularly useful item to make is a purpose-designed box to house specific items of equipment and, unlike the items previously described, this cannot always be purchased. It is possible to buy a variety of plastic boxes but these are more vulnerable to breakage than timber and rarely the correct size. The high cost of labour has seen the end of the exquisitely built wooden containers which are now mainly replaced by mass-production plastic. Gun cases are a good example. My double guns live in an oak double-gun case with hardly discernible joints, lined with deep red baize and covered externally with an excellent light brown leather, obviously built by a craftsman. The corners are of thick brass and to protect it against the bruises of life the whole lives in an outer covering of thick canvas. To buy such a case now would cost more than a top quality London gun cost before the war.

Not that I am suggesting that you or I can make such a case; I am merely lamenting the death of craftsmanship on the spear of inflation. But it is possible to produce a workmanlike job which will serve as well or better than a bought article and cost much less. For example, I recently bought a double-barrel ·410 for our third son, who had progressed from beater to shooting man overnight. Having no case I made one from oddments lying around the workshop, plus a few items costing, literally, pence. The lid and base were cut from ply and edged with 2 in. × ¾ in. soft wood on the base and 1 in. × ¾ in. on the lid, giving an internal depth of 3 in. The exterior faces were covered with green canvas (used in the productive years to cover dismantled cots and other baby-rearing equipment being conveyed northwards on a car roof), with the edges being carried well down the inside faces of the case edges. Next the interior was partitioned in soft wood to suit the components of the gun, and the whole interior then lined with ½ in.-thick foam-plastic sheet. Hinges were fitted by putting in only one screw on each face until they were correctly positioned. The handle and closing catches came from a luggage shop and finally the corners were made from leather obtained by shaving the hair off an old red deer hide.

The result was a light, durable, cheap and presentable case and the same principle can be used for a variety of equipment. Fishing tackle is particularly vulnerable to breakage and easily lost and is best housed in a decent container. I made one some years ago which is a foot deep and divided into two levels by a tray. The bottom section is deeper and contains the reels and other larger items while such things as fly boxes live on top. As the whole of the exterior facing was ply on a soft-wood frame I stained the wood to bring out the grain and then waxed it. (Avoid the various polyurethane varnish finishes which look marvellous when first applied but are most difficult to remove when drab and scratched. No one has yet devised a better finish for wood than wax and hard work.) Here again the interior was lined with foam-plastic sheet which not only provides a perfect shock absorbing lining for delicate equipment but completely hides any minor imperfections of workmanship from critical friends.

Personally I have never been able to resist buying fly boxes, but, for those who can, an old cigar box lined with foam sheet does the job perfectly. It is, in fact, superior to the expensive metal versions where the fly is clamped under a small flexible metal bar, thereby distorting the shape. (For those who have not discovered them, Messrs. Hardy's sell the the best fly boxes currently available. Light and cheap, these are made of plastic with ridges of an inverted 'V' shape along the floors of the lid and base. The sharp edge of the 'V' opens to take the hook and the fly is held firmly with the dressing clear of any contact. A wind will not empty the box and if you drop it in the river it floats.)

Floats are a good subject for the handy-man for they are easily made and quite expensive to purchase. I am fortunate in having access, in a roundabout way, to a Dorset peacock which provides me with occasional tail feathers. The quill makes floats and the herl produces a most effective dark nymph which does great things with our local lake trout when fished slowly in the surface film at dusk. A good live bait float for pike can be made by inserting a thin plastic tube through a table tennis ball and painting one half red.

Spinners are becoming expensive items, especially if, like me, you fish with young sons and daughters who tend to hook everything solid on the far bank. (After getting rather cross with them at the loss of seven spinners in one morning in the Hebrides this last summer, I hooked a heifer on the back cast with a salmon tube fly. The heifer got excited and the family, who have a very warped sense of humour, offered me advice and encouragement while I played it.) An excellent solution is to make spoons from brass sheet. The thickness of the sheet will be determined by the weight of lure you need, and the wisest course is to produce spoons of varying thicknesses to cope with various water conditions. Make a template of the shape you require, scribe it onto the brass sheet and cut it out with metal shears. Then tap away at one side only with a small, round-head hammer. The surface under attack will rapidly assume a concave shape and the small dents of the hammer blows add a scale-like finish. Drill a hole at either end and fit split rings, one for a swivel and the other for the treble hook. Finally, if you believe the theory that red on a bait suggests the blood of a wounded fish and attracts predatory fish, add a diagonal stripe of red paint. These spoons can be made in any size from midgets for small trout to monsters for pike and spring salmon. They have the advantage, unlike some commercial lures, that a few minutes with a soft cloth and metal polish restores all the original sparkle.

A fundamental rule of all equipment and tackle is that it must be both simple and practical. This is well illustrated by two examples of home-made clothing I have met with. The first is familiar to all countrymen and is the simple expedient of the beaters, facing wet cover, who tie plastic agricultural sacks around their legs. Simple and practical. The second example was supplied by an inventive friend who turned up for a wet day at driven grouse with a home-made hat shaped like an inverted saucer and fashioned from wire and plastic sheet. It was so wide that the rain dribbling off the perimeter fell wide of his shoulders and he was much envied at our assembly point on the low ground. Unfortunately it failed to stand a field test for, as we climbed onto the high ground, the first decent gust of wind threatened to strangle him with the chin strap. Simple but impractical.

While it is enormously satisfying to conceive and produce new items of equipment it is also beneficial to go to some trouble to ensure you derive the best service from existing tackle. In fact some measures take only seconds but could have important consequences—for example, the care of monofilament line. Spare spools should not be left jostling in the bottom of the fishing bag with scissors, gags and disgorgers but kept in a protective bag. Monofilament deteriorates faster in strong light and is better kept in the dark. It is also good practice to write the date on each spool as you purchase it and use the oldest line first. Finally wetting the line before knotting prevents bruising and increases knot strength. It is sufficient to tie the knot loosely and then suck it for a few few seconds before drawing it tight, slowly but firmly. With interchangeable spools a convenient way of keeping the line in position and remembering the breaking strain is to knot a wide elastic band in the centre, slip one loop over the spool and label the second loop with the line strength.

Another example of a little trouble possibly attracting a major reward is the trick of carrying a small block of fine carborundum stone in the fishing bag. A few strokes on a less-than-keen hook point could be critical.

There are other wrinkles. Thin-wall plastic rainwater pipes

make superb rod carriers and cost very little. On long days by the water it is less tiring to carry your fishing bag by looping it to a stout waist-belt than slinging it over a shoulder. Preparing dead baits in a hurry just before setting off is always a nuisance and makes for poor workmanship. There is no need, for the work can be done months before and the baits popped in a deep freeze until needed. (*All* fishing and shooting men should have a deep freeze.)

The list of possibilities is endless and it is pointless for me to go on. If you are already a tackle tinkerer you do not need me. If you are not I have by now either converted you or lost your interest. But, if you come in the latter group, next time a rotten string breaks and your duck decoys drift away on the tide, or a rusty swivel loses you a salmon, you may imagine you hear a faint, wicked chuckle. It will be me.

CHAPTER SEVEN

HAPPY THE KEEPER

It would not be unreasonable to claim that a man with the character and personality to make a good keeper would not make a bad Prime Minister—indeed, he could make rather a good one. Both jobs call for patience, tact, tenacity, foresight, leadership, the ability to shrug off failure, masses of common sense and a strong vein of cunning, although in politicians this quality is more kindly referred to as shrewdness. Both keepers and Prime Ministers also share the occupational hazard that if they fail to get results they are sacked. Keepers are more vulnerable than Prime Ministers in that they can be removed much more quickly, but then they enjoy the advantages that it is far easier for them to find a similar position elsewhere. A further advantage keepers have over senior politicians is that the public do not expect them to maintain high moral standards. In fact, the reverse applies, for the profession gained something of a name with the publicity given to *Lady Chatterley's Lover*, and I not infrequently come across a member upholding this reputation. Perhaps it's all the fresh air. Or it may be the examples paraded before them, for keepers' coverts and fields are frequently invaded by courting couples at the season of the year when keepers move around quietly. For many years I shot pigeons each February and March in Cambridgeshire and my contact was a keeper who went to much trouble to erect suitable hides for me prior to my visits. Being a sociable character who led a rather solitary existence he would spend part of each day with me in the hide and after we had dealt with the season's bag of pheasants and the current feeding habits of the pigeons, he would turn to his observations of the last summer's crop of lovers. More than one pigeon owed its life to approaching the decoys at the moment that he was recounting the more lurid details of some amorous escapade.

The best instance I can offer of the influence of the fair sex on keepers comes from a personal example a couple of seasons ago. I took a Gun in a Hampshire shoot and started the season with high hopes. Unfortunately the results were, to put it kindly, disappointing. We began with small, weak birds and by the time the survivors were full grown the majority had strayed. Clearly the keeper had erred and the syndicate captain made no attempt to protect him in the circular letter he sent to the Guns at the end of the season soliciting their support for the coming year. In a phrase that could have come straight from Dickens, he wrote, 'XYZ started well but fell victim, as single keepers do, to a wretched woman.' The danger is not, of course, confined purely to keepers, but they are perhaps more vulnerable than most as the season of the year when wretched women are most demanding happens to clash with the heavy task of rearing and, as XYZ found, there is not time to attend to the needs of both.

In spite of this serious risk it has long been my sincerely held belief that the lot of the keeper is a happy one. In fact, I will go further and declare that if ever I make some grave error of judgement and my business crumbles to the point where, penniless and discarded by my profession, I have to seek a new job I will, without hesitation, become a gamekeeper. Not for me the noise and boredom of a factory production line screwing the same unchanging things onto a motor car, or sitting in a booking office selling train tickets to a dull, grey stream of humans, half of them suffering from wet, noisy colds. And then going home across the concrete, asphalt and the city smells to an airless, characterless box, or even part of a box. Why should I suffer a completely unnatural existence when I could be outdoors with the weather on my face and a degree of responsibility and independence that office workers only command as they reach senior positions.

Consider the advantages. There are many but the greatest is that of living in the countryside and among country people. Because civilization is now so sophisticated we are unable to see the enormous wood for the massive trees and it is not as obvious as it should be that we are going slightly mad. In our defence there is not a lot we can do about it. The system catches us up, educates us, channels us neatly into our specialist occupations, treats our ills, moulds our buying habits, holidays, clothes, speech—everything in the way we live and die becomes increasingly part of a set pattern. It is impossible to condemn any single feature—the power of a trade union to cause grave inconvenience to the public can be defended. So can the noise endured by the many so that a few can travel quickly by air. There is a case for permitting motor-cars to choke cities, and countless other activities of dubious value can offer a logical defence. But when one stands back and looks at the total picture it is difficult not to conclude, I repeat, that we are going a little mad. Until, that is, one enters the countryside and returns to a world of sanity. A world where the weather forecast preceding the news is of greater importance than the news itself. Where, in spite of modern pressures, common sense still prevails and people do not exaggerate the worth of material possessions whose value lies more in the act of possession rather than their utility. Living on the doorstep of nature and watching the rhythm of the seasons makes even the most poorly educated of men a minor philosopher. My old Norfolk uncle left school at thirteen and laboured on the land for the next half-century. He has a sense of responsibility, a willingness to help others without reward and a fund of practical common sense that is frequently missing in the city dweller of much wider horizons and education.

Perhaps the difference between town and country is caused by the town dweller losing contact with the fundamental things of life—earth, growing crops, animals, weather—and in the process also losing the peace and content of the countryside. I forget the name of the researcher, and the value of his work deserves better, who investigated the effect on rats of confining them in unnaturally high densities. He concluded that the more rats are packed together the more their normally good social behaviour breaks down and such sins as robbery, rape and violence increase. He could have foretold this by studying the crime figures for any big city.

These advantages of environment and work are enjoyed by the keeper to the full. Not only is he in the countryside but it is his job to observe in detail, unlike the tractor driver who is constantly watching his furrow or the dairyman among his endless tubes and humming machinery. The keeper has the creative pleasure of using tools, and the basic pleasure of rearing creatures. When, on early summer mornings with my business acquaintances still abed, I have done watering and feeding my pheasants I lean on the pen and watch them. I see them strong and lithe, with the colours of the young cocks beginning to glow, and I think of them as they were a few weeks ago when I could hold half a dozen fluffy bundles in the cup of my hands. And I know how my farming friends feel when they lean on a gate and look at their corn or cattle.

Countrymen seem to produce more and richer characters than townsmen and these form part of the keeper's world. At the top end of the social scale he will meet, and on reasonably pleasant terms, a great range of shooting guests. Given an employer who travels widely to shoot he will see more of the country in a season than many men in a lifetime. Modest opportunities for sport will come to him, if only flighting pigeons or ferreting, and he may even be able to offer sport to his friends. Many keepers are virtually their own bosses, left in peace by their employers to work the hours they choose with the sole proviso that there is ample sport in the season. The counter reply to this heads the list of the job's disadvantages—that at certain times of the year it is necessary to work long hours. This I grant, but it is a rare keeper who does not enjoy free time to compensate— picking-up or beating elsewhere, attending Crufts, and other pleasurable activities.

The need to be out in all weathers is often quoted as a disadvantage. I cannot agree. It seems a far better fate to me to have to be outdoors on most days of the year than to be compelled to remain indoors on most days—which is the plight of the majority. Poor pay is the greatest complaint and there is much justice in this grumble. In fact it is often better than it seems for the job usually provides a cottage and after the town dweller has paid the rent or mortgage on his home he will often have very little more of his wages left than the keeper. Nor does he have the opportunities that come to country dwellers for cheap eggs, vegetables, fruit for picking and the like. I will not dwell on the subject of tipping in case some sporting member of the Inland Revenue reads this and writes to correct me pointing out that, according to keepers' tax returns, the practice died out some years ago.

It is arguable that the keeper has always enjoyed a more favourable job than his fellows, although the work was undeniably harder a century ago. My evidence comes from Richard Jefferies' classic *The Gamekeeper at Home*, which was first published in 1879 and which so vividly portrays the flavour of the men and the times that I will quote from it several times in this chapter. If you can find a copy anywhere obtain it by almost any means. On the debit side he recorded, 'The keeper is often about the best part of the night.' I wonder how many of today's keepers miss more than the occasional night's sleep. And where the modern keeper simply telephones for several tons of his favoured pheasant rearing food the old-timer 'has his own specific treatment, in which he has implicit faith, and laughs to scorn the pheasant-meals and feeding-stuffs advertised in the papers. He mixes it himself, and likes no one prying about to espy his secret.' Times were harsher and on the subject of violence he wrote, 'Scarcely a keeper can be found who has not got one or more tales to tell of encounters with poachers, sometimes of a desperate character,' and 'The raiders who come in gangs armed with guns and shoot in the preserves, are usually the scum of the manufacturing towns.'

Most of the keepers of my acquaintance are the most excellent men, but not all, for the lack of supervision makes the job attractive to the idle and dishonest. (To quote Jefferies once more, 'Gamekeeping is an occupation peculiarly favourable to loafing if a man is inclined that way.') Every February sees a crop of casualties from these causes, although keepers are also at risk from unreasonable employers who blame them for unavoidable losses. Drink is a great temptation for the weak keeper, for the opportunities they can bestow on their fellows make them great favourites at the bar. Simple idleness is a greater pitfall for keepers than most men, for in most jobs a failure to achieve results is quickly obvious and a smart shove will often correct the offender when he has only lagged a little. But keepers' shortcomings are often only detected after some months, usually when shooting begins and redress is impossible. The embarrassment is not always confined to the keeper. I once had the opportunity of renting, with a friend, a grouse moor in northwest Yorkshire. It had come by chance into the hands of a company in which a mutual friend was a director. He knew nothing of grouse or shooting but invited us to take a lease, mentioning that the grouse had been unshot for several years but that the old keeper was still retained on a part-time basis. We arranged an inspection and duly arrived at the moor and met the keeper. Alf, as I will call him, was every inch a Yorkshire keeper of the old school. What he knew, and we did not, was that over the years the moor had gone steadily downhill. The heather of the adjoining moors had gone before a heavy invasion of sheep and now our moor was a small oasis of heather in a desert of grass. With little or no active keepering the farmers had exceeded their sheep 'gates', the vermin had multiplied and the grouse diminished. But Alf had no intention of saying so for we represented full employment once more. We were taken to the most prolific area, grouse were shown and tales of the good old days

94

revived. Fired with enthusiasm we leased the ground, elevated Alf, both in status and financial reward, to full-time keeper, formed an eight-Gun syndicate and waited anxiously for August. For good measure we arranged for Alf to buy in two hundred day-old pheasant chicks and rear and release these in a wooded valley that probed like a pointing finger from the low ground up towards the moor. Meanwhile my friends on the *Shooting Times* came to hear of the venture and, wishing to report on this attempt to revive an old moor, arranged for one of their staff and a photographer to join us on the 12th. Came the great day and a large assembly gathered at the foot of the hill—Guns, wives and other hangers-on, the keeper, and all the hill farmers of the area and their sons who were to beat.

The Guns moved into the butts, loaded and tensed. The beaters disappeared over the horizon, and all was quiet but for the bees. Forty minutes' later the beaters reached the butts and not a grouse had been seen. Alf said the hot weather had sent them to the higher ground where it was cooler. On the next drive we saw three. By lunch we had shot four. The Guns were looking hard at me; I was looking even harder at Alf and the men from the *Shooting Times* were looking depressed. At the end the bag was seven and a snipe and Alf said he simply couldn't understand it. Dinner was a quiet affair except for the occasional suggestion that the birds might have concentrated on tomorrow's ground. The morning quickly proved they had not and by the time we pulled the beer bottles out of the stream by the lunch hut the total bag was eleven. (We had quickly learnt not to count our grouse in braces.) Alf still couldn't understand it. 'It' might have been, he volunteered, disease, or hikers, or the late snow, or dogs from the village or almost anything except the fact that the grouse were not there when we took the moor and had not been there for years.

In spite of the paucity of birds we loved the surroundings and the occasional sport but the final blow came in November when we lined the bottom of the valley and sent the beaters to come through from the head for the grand *battue* at the pheasants. One, one out of two hundred, appeared. Alf couldn't understand that either but I learnt the truth later. He was not over popular locally, not least because he was a foreigner to the dale having only moved there some thirty years previously. The locals, feeling no need to protect him, had waited until he fattened the pheasants and then poached them.

My parting with Alf was done gently, for although he had cost me money, time and some embarrassment, he had my sympathy. We adjusted our methods, expenditure and expectations to reality and shot the moor for several more years. A lot of pleasure came from it, but sometimes as I stood in a butt looking across a barren moor I would conjure up a vision of Alf saying, 'Ay—I've seen't time ween't birds coom across that beck like snowflakes.'

In contrast one finds men like Charlie South, till his recent retirement Head Keeper on a famous Cambridgeshire estate, having succeeded his father before him. Short, quiet, cap on head, round featured with alert eyes that missed nothing, Charlie held sway over some of the best shooting in England for years. Nothing appeared to trouble him. I recall a hare shoot on a February day when the wind was bitter but a bright sun shone. On such occasions the Head Keeper is a minor Napoleon commanding a mixed army of tractor drivers, estate workers, farmers, Cambridge students who had pinched a day from their lectures, and others making up a shooting motley. The problem is to encircle and eventually execute a considerable number of alert hares over several hundred acres of ground. On this particular day Charlie had blundered and after two hours of hard walking by all involved a flank had failed to close and the enemy had streamed out to freedom. The Guns were grouped together conducting a post-mortem with the embittered air of farmers who have sown assiduously but failed to reap, when the General's car, in the form of Charlie's Land-Rover, appeared. The more voluble leapt at him with a torrent of complaint. Charlie, impassive, listened for a minute then held up one hand. Silence fell. 'It is', said Charlie, quietly, 'far too nice a day to squabble—let's get on with the next drive.' And they did.

The funniest keeper I ever met was a stalker on Mull; a tall, lean Scotsman, with a permanent twinkle in his eye and a background of forty years' service on the same ground to add to the forty-two years of his father. Colin was born in an isolated cottage at the foot of Glen More (it was through this glen that Robert Louis Stevenson had David Balfour tramp, in the novel *Kidnapped*, after he was cast ashore at Erraid). The glen rises to Ben More, the highest hill on Mull and the slopes were dotted with the red deer which are his interest and work. To Colin, in the course of a season, come many men in pursuit of the deer; some novices, some experienced, some fit, some most unfit. Whatever their category the same rule applies—that the Gun must go to the deer for the deer cannot be brought to the Gun. The resultant adventures of men toiling up and down the hills of Mull would make a good book. To gain their full flavour they must be heard in his soft brogue as he sits by a peat fire. I like the tale of a novice who, after a long stalk, Colin took to within forty yards of a stag. 'Tak him noo,' whispered Colin, handing him the rifle. 'Right,' said the novice and promptly stood up, to aim better. 'The beast,' recalls Colin, 'couldn't have stopped before he reached Oban.' Then there is the tale of a new ghillie, an Irishman and unfamiliar with the job. In due course a stag was shot and he was invited to drag it down to the nearest access point for the pony. 'Not until you cut the —— horns off,' he replied.

I like keepers as a race. Perhaps the reason is a subliminal longing to do the job brought on by a quarter of a century of intense business pressure in the property world of south-east England. There are, after all, no telephones, planning committees, completion deadlines, or compulsory purchase orders for motorways, intervening in the eminently more practical business of converting an egg into a pheasant poult. More obvious factors are the characters that have been forged by the nature of their work or, put rather better by Richard Jefferies, 'He meets your eye full and unshirkingly, yet without insolence; not yet as the labourers do, who either stare with sullen ill-will or look at the earth. In brief, freedom and constant contact with nature have made him every inch a man.' My liking for keepers coupled with my interest in all aspects of their work, has led to both some good friendships over the years and many enjoyable experiences.

Some of my best contacts with keepers have been forged along the Norfolk coast where I have a farmer friend who, gentleman that he is, invites me to a couple of days' formal driven shooting each winter. Some years ago he phoned to suggest I brought double guns as the pheasants had done well. I replied that I had no loader. No matter, he said, a loader could be found. Came the morning and I met my loader who, to avoid him any embarrassment, I will call Tom. Then in his early thirties, broad shouldered and with the alert look found in those men whose life is spent anticipating the misdeeds of others, he looked a very solid citizen. Time has proved the accuracy of that assessment. Delicate questioning showed he was a special constable, the secretary of the local wildfowlers' club, and had a range of interests that included producing and marketing his own brand of honey. All told in the Norfolk dialect which, to me, is one of the most pleasing of local tongues.

I shot, he loaded, and at the end of the day I had 81 head to my credit and an invitation to flight wigeon under the moon that night. Since then Tom and I have had some grand hours, both by day and night, fowling along the Norfolk coast. When we wait for the tide to move or dusk to fall we shelter in a creek or under the sea wall and talk of guns, dogs and much else. The next morning we may each be involved in a formal driven shoot—him as a beater and me as a Gun.

Through Tom my acquaintance with the Norfolk keepers developed and thereby my experience of the countryside was enriched. To return, for an instant, to my earlier theme, this small group of men lead lives which are, in some respects, hard but are also varied, interesting and infinitely more rewarding than those who work indoors at monotonous tasks. One amusing fact which emerged from odd comments picked up among the various friendships I formed is an appreciation of how much beaters observe. I had never made the mistake of thinking that the silent group of plastic-coated Norfolk

men, with fertilizer sacks tied round their legs with binder
twine, were concerned solely with disturbing pheasants into
the air and were indifferent, or oblivious to all else. But I had
not previously realized that every single detail of the day was
noted, weighed and discussed. Who is invited and who is left
out. Which Gun is shooting well and which not. How young
Charles shot too close to Mr. Duke, the look he got and what
his father said. Whose wife came for lunch every day last
season but has only come once this. Nothing is missed,
particularly, human nature being no less present in agri-
culturalists, those things detrimental to those they dislike
and those things favourable to those they like.

In due time I was honoured by a regular invitation to the
end-of-the-season keepers' shoot in Norfolk, an event
beginning in great good humour all round only to ascend to
an even happier level after lunch in the local pub. The study
of the unspoken barriers that are erected between men who
have placed themselves in different classes are a source of
constant pleasure to me and one of these days provided an
amusing instance. Arriving with my Norfolk farmer friend
the previous evening I was told, with a certain pleasurable
malice, that while I would be shooting on one estate with the
keepers he would be shooting on the next with the landowners. I pointed out that he could hardly have expected
any better of me, being a man who kept a spaniel in preference to a labrador. Next day we went our separate ways,
not expecting to meet again until dinner, only to find in the
late morning the two parties converging on one small lane
dividing the two estates. For the connoisseur of people it
was a great moment as each party went about its business as
if the other never existed. We, that is the keepers and other
lesser beings, were lining the edge of a wood which formed
our boundary prior to driving it out to our comrades on the
far side. The gentlemen moved into position in the adjoining
field, facing a wood on the opposite side. Just as we were
poised to move off a gun fired twice in the field and a cock
pheasant appeared over our wood, no doubt chuckling at
having safely crossed the firing line once more. There are no
niceties at a keepers' shoot and it was not so much a question

of whether he would be shot at as who would get him first. I think two Guns shared him but I wouldn't say the claim of the third man was without merit. By common consent the keepers' line about faced towards the field and not a bird missed by the gentlemen survived the keepers.

At dinner that night I felt it wisest not only to let my host raise the matter first but even to sound surprised. It was, I explained to him, a very thick wood.

Not the least pleasant men to be found in the keepering world are those concerned with water, but then who could spend all his working hours beside a river and not have his philosophy improved. Once, exploring the remoter parts of the Outer Hebrides, I came across a man who had tried and proved my belief that most of us would be happier working outdoors. 'Robin', to continue with nom de plumes, had once been an estate agent on the south coast of England. He was also not only a typically enthusiastic fisherman but skilled to the extent of having represented Wales in international championships. One day he spotted an advertisement for an experienced man to run a fishery in the Hebrides and, as he told me in earnest detail, felt it would be beneficial not just for himself but for his wife and family to take the job just for a year. When I met him he was part way through the fourth and my judgement is that he will still be there years hence.

It would be gratifying to believe that most keepers are pleasant fellows because contact with the countryside has made them so. Conversely it may be that the work attracts men of good quality. The truth, I suspect, is a combination; that men who seek country work have their values right and contact with nature puts on a final polish.

The cynic may argue that as keepers represent one of the last outposts of tipping, it pays them to be pleasant. Although I rarely see such considerations influence the attitude of my taxi drivers I will concede that keepers are rarely absent when the Guns are leaving and most shooting men will have frantically searched through their pockets finding only a penknife, cartridges and about seventy yards of string, as the keeper works his way among the Guns, his arms festooned with pheasants and murmuring to each man,

'I picked a nice brace for you, sir.' There are even one or two sour keepers of my acquaintance where I consider the tip well spent just for the pleasure of watching them, for a few minutes at the end of each day, force upon an unwilling face a strange expression which they believe represents a mixture of pleasure that the gentlemen have had a good day tinged with regret at their departure.

But who can blame the keeper for seeking what is just extra income to which, by long tradition, he is entitled. Not I, for tipping becomes less as the private employers grow fewer and more keepers work for syndicates. The man who has paid £1,000 for a season's shooting, and it is difficult now to arrange matters for less, is far less inclined to tip the keeper generously than a guest Gun who has had a good day's sport for nothing. Times have indeed changed since Richard Jefferies wrote, 'The keeper is one of those fortunate individuals who all the world tip.'

There is some art in the act of receiving a tip and a Gun is rarely left in doubt if he has been too careful. (The reverse does not apply.) For the overcautious tipper the 'Thank you, sir' will still be forthcoming but it will be hung with signs for all but the dull-witted. The voice may fall on the 'sir', the gift will be pocketed rapidly as if the recipient is trying to hide it from public view to save the donor embarrassment, eyes do not meet, and the keeper does not linger to discuss the day. One of my head keeper friends, whose identity must be carefully hidden, was once told by his boss that the son of an E.I.P. (exceptionally important person) was coming to shoot. He came, he shot for two days and at the end my friend, mentally picturing at least a couple of fivers, said he hoped Sir had enjoyed himself. Sir said he had, thanked him and gave him a ten shilling note. My friend returned to the under keepers and by common consent the gift was framed. In defence of Sir, who was very young and anyway probably had little idea of the value of money, I wish to record that I do not think he was mean by nature but someone should have made sure he knew the facts of life before he was sent out into the world.

This sad tale serves to illustrate that the greater art in

tipping is not receiving but giving. There are noisy tippers, furtive tippers, arrogant tippers, embarrassed tippers—tippers of all varieties. The greatest artists are those where no money is seen to change hands. A brief conversation in a quiet corner of the yard, a slight movement around waist level and each goes about his business content. Farmers are very good at this; no doubt because they are closer to the keeper than most. Of course you can still find keepers who have no fancy ideas about dignity and would rather have a large tip proffered badly than a small one presented delicately. There was a Norfolk keeper who, after I had departed from a shooting visit, said to his boss, 'Thar't Mr. Marchington's a roight gentleman.' Taken aback by such a gross error of judgement my farmer friend could only ask why—'Er giv me a foiver.'

What does the future hold for our keeper friends? It is difficult to be optimistic for on the one hand the costs of running a shoot rise and on the other heavy taxation and the increasing cost of living leave men less to spare for pleasure. These factors were responsible for the birth of syndicates in the last century, when individual estate owners begun to find the cost of giving shooting hospitality to their friends too great. Now the syndicates are in the majority and they are finding increasing difficulty in keeping subscriptions within reasonable limits. In spite of this I think the profession will survive for men have a knack of solving the problems threatening those things they enjoy. I certainly hope so for without keepers the countryside would be a duller place.

CHAPTER EIGHT

DOGS OF MY ACQUAINTANCE

The relationship established between men and dogs over the centuries is much loved by authors, writers of TV documentaries and the like. The situations and settings vary from amiable St. Bernards fighting through blizzards with liquid salvation around their necks to sheepdogs performing flawlessly to the piercing whistles of the shepherds. In all cases the theme is constant—of our canine friends giving their selfless all to serve their human masters. Applying this touching picture to the world of gundogs should produce a scene of dignified labradors sitting obediently at heel while pheasants fall all around; of spaniels tenaciously beating out thick bramble and dropping instantly to shot; pointers set in rock-like points on distant moors; and dogs of various breeds making long-distance retrieves of wildfowl across the saltings.

Now I am sure that there exist really excellent dogs who are reliable performers; it has just been my misfortune to come across them only at rare intervals. I am frequently introduced to dogs who were very good but are now too old; dogs who will be very good but are yet too young; excellent dogs who have been put off for the day by the delicate condition of that springer bitch over there; really first-class dogs who are, surprisingly, off form today; outstanding dogs who haven't worked for several weeks and are rusty; superb dogs who happen never to perform well in heather/roots/stubble or whatever the cover of the day happens to be. All these I have seen and many more but rarely a good dog actually performing as a good dog.

The truth is not far to seek. Apart from keepers and professional trainers almost no one has the time to spare necessary to train a dog to a high standard and maintain it there. My springer was trained by rising at 5.30 a.m. and working on an adjoining common where there is little game and consequently little scent. This worked during the summer but in the winter I had to be in my office practically at dawn and training was restricted to the week-end, which was already full. The great majority of shooting men share my predicament and the outcome is to be seen in the large number of imperfect dogs. And even if we all had time the truth is that few men have the ability. A few seconds' thought will show that dog training must be a very skilled occupation but, undaunted, the great variety of men who make up the shooting world select a puppy and set to the task of training it with touching confidence. The outcome produces the interesting situation in which there are either bad dogs or good dogs—never bad amateur trainers and good amateur trainers. Or, put another way, if the outcome is a good dog then the owner modestly accepts credit. If the result is a bad dog then the faults were inherent in the breeding.

Sending a dog away for training is only a partial solution. I have a keeper friend who once trained what promised to be an outstanding labrador. It caught the eye of a wealthy sportsman from Liverpool who invited the keeper to name his price and was asked for, and paid, £300. (In those days a high figure.) Prior to the conclusion of the deal the dog was thoroughly demonstrated and was flawless. Within four months it was back for a refresher course, for the new owner had assumed it was a form of canine gramophone record which could be played at will and left in a case in between.

It was while this chapter was being written that I was lent

a copy of Talbot Radcliffe's *Spaniels for Sport*, published by Faber & Faber, based on H. W. Carlton's classic and a most excellent book of instruction. The foreword was by Wilson Stephens, Editor of *The Field*, whose writings fill me with admiration and depression. Admiration because he is so very good and depression because while I lumber at the construction of sentences and ideas, his work obviously flows elegantly off the tip of a restless pen. Explaining why it was necessary for the book to be rewritten to adapt it to the time available to modern amateur trainers he wrote, 'The limitless time, the unthinkability that business might ever interfere with pleasure, the spacious backgrounds in which no man lacked paddocks nor access to coverts well stocked with whatever game the lesson of the moment demanded. From sunrise to sundown nothing of the workaday world seemed to intrude upon a man intent upon training a spaniel.'

Although the various authoritative books on dog training will set out, in entrancingly simple terms, the procedures necessary to produce an excellent dog, happiness will only come from realizing that for those who are restricted both by their own ability and the quality of their dog, which is to say the great majority, it is impossible to achieve perfection. Someone once wrote that a man could play a bad game of golf yet still be a gentleman and a good father. A dog can possess various imperfections and still be a great character and a lovable companion. The art is to cultivate the frame of mind where if you find yourselves shooting with men who are critical of your dog's every misdemeanour you automatically think of changing your companions rather than your dog. Once you cease to long for perfection the little misfortunes of the day will fall into perspective. I well recall acting as a stop Gun at the end of a long Sussex wood. Nothing much happened for a while and then a hare crashed through closely followed by one of the other Guns' labradors. They quickly disappeared over the horizon and it was with some reluctance that I told him the news, fearing to cause embarrassment. Far from looking uncomfortable he was almost offhand. 'Oh, he won't go far—the river's only another half-mile.'

One of the many bonuses of the sport of shooting, enjoyed by all keepers and beaters and the more observant Guns, is the pleasure of watching other dog owners failing to control their dogs under practical field conditions. The owners' reactions to this embarrassing situation depends upon whether they blame failure on the dog or themselves. Those who blame the dog are usually wrong but give greater pleasure to their fellows. (Napoleon summed it up rather well although not I confess with gundogs in mind, when he said, 'There are no such things as bad soldiers just bad officers'.) One naturally expects the worst examples of dog behaviour to come from the dogs of novice owners. A case that comes to mind concerns walking up grouse with a friend from the south who arrived at the moor with his new labrador, fresh from training in a Home Counties garden. Various adventures of no great interest occurred until the moment when I dropped a grouse over a hillock and out of sight. Hercules, as I had named him as the result of a strong facial resemblance to Steptoe and Son's horse, lumbered off, unbidden, and a long pause ensued. Eventually he reappeared, carrying the grouse. 'He's got it,' called the proud owner somewhat unnecessarily. He had indeed. He had 'got it' so well that its intestines were flying on either side of its head like streamers in the wind. I suggested it might be best to finish gutting it before we proceeded and sat on a peat hag and did the job. Regrettably I failed to make my point.

A great bond exists between most men and their dogs, and this affection is not related to the ability of the animal for men love the bad dogs as much as the good. Perhaps the reason is that dogs are all that we wish humans would be; completely devoted to us; blind to our faults; giving us their complete attention and devoid of all malice and deceit. We have no need to maintain false standards or stand on our dignity with a dog. Life comes down to simple needs and satisfactions and, resting in Hebridean heather with a view across the Minch and my spaniel and a brace of grouse beside me, the dog and I enjoy a perfect relationship. Just how much she reasons and anticipates I cannot be sure, but she gives me an affection and loyalty that is without limit, and in turn I think more of her than it is wise for a man to do of an animal.

It is no rare thing to see strong stern men, who can run a factory or a large office without allowing sentiment to influence their decisions, relax into the softest of men with their dogs. Many would not admit it, but the feeling is there and can be seen in many small things. I recall on a bitter January day's shooting in Norfolk last winter, watching an exceptionally large farmer with an exceptionally small spaniel. The obvious love of the pair for one another was touching. The most practical demonstration also occurred in Norfolk, when I was wildfowling with a friend and his large black labrador. When we were returning and still nearly two miles from the car the dog was taken ill and had obvious difficulty in walking. Without hesitation he lifted it around his neck and carried it like a child. My pleasure at this was marred by the obligation I felt to offer to carry his gun and equipment which, with my own, made a substantial load. I was tempted to offer to carry the dog instead!

I have never had any illusions about my own liking for dogs. After all, what can one expect from a man who at the age of fourteen wept when the vet gently ruled that an aged ferret should be put down. But I never fully appreciated the depth of feeling that develops until my first spaniel was killed by a lorry on a minor road whilst retrieving a cock pheasant. It was fortunate it was almost the end of the season for I had no stomach for shooting for several months.

Although one reads frequent stories of the ill-treatment of dogs, I think these rarely occur with owners of sporting dogs. Such behaviour is mainly confined to those who have no real use for a dog and if asked why they kept one would be unable to give a solid reason. In support of this view I have the fact that in all the years I have only twice seen men beat shooting dogs. The first was, somewhat appropriately, a beater at a Hampshire shoot whom I have since referred to as the Winchester Whacker. The case was straightforward enough. The beaters were strung out across a series of water meadows and were 'brushing' them towards the standing Guns. The

Whacker had a labrador with him and when the beaters had
almost reached the Guns it ran into a shot pheasant. He
promptly caught it and thrashed it brutally with a stick.
The point of the story is not the act but the reaction of the
onlookers who were by then all fairly close observers. The
fashion in which a group of people can instantly develop an
atmosphere and form a common attitude of disapproval is
seen daily, ranging from such situations as a foul on a football
field to a gaffe at a dinner table. On this occasion everyone froze and stared with expressions ranging from embarrassment to open hostility. So far as I know he was never
employed again.

The other occasion was almost unique in that I watched a
man beat another man's dog before his eyes. This was a
keeper on a Yorkshire grouse moor where one of my fellow
Guns owned a big yellow labrador which wanted to kill
everything on four legs and had reservations about most
things on two. Other dogs of any size, sheep and even cattle
were all regarded as enemies to be subdued and he waged
war most successfully, oblivious to the whistle and com-
mands of his owner. The keeper took a dislike to the dog and
would mutter audible criticisms of the beast and its training
to no one in particular, invariably ending with the view that
he needed a good hiding. There the situation would have
rested but for the arrival of Snipe, a spaniel belonging to
another Gun. Snipe was old but with a knack of curling one
lip, exposing a fang and snarling, which suggested that in
his day he had stood no nonsense. He and the labrador
instantly hated one another but their experienced owners
kept them apart until one lunch break on the moor. Con-
cerning themselves rather too much with the beer and
sandwiches they forgot the dogs until a noise that would
have made a superb background to a Tarzan film announced
the outbreak of war. Human spectators in a dog fight divide
sharply into those who think they can do something to stop
it and those who have no intention of trying. The dogs not
having won a popular following, the optimists on this
occasion were limited to the owners who showed no great
enthusiasm for putting their hands into the canine equivalent

of a mincing machine. They quickly stood back whereupon the keeper advanced with his stick and began to beat the combatants apart. It seemed a straightforward situation until I realized that every blow fell upon the hated yellow labrador and the spaniel was untouched. Being untouched it fought on, which obliged the labrador to continue and in turn permitted the keeper to go on beating. It was an embarrassing scene and difficult to halt.

The strangest instance I ever encountered of a dog with a fault and the owner's acceptance of it happened with a wildfowling friend and his labrador, a large, black beast of an unusually quiet and introspective disposition. When I first began to shoot with them I was puzzled by the fact that my companion invariably ended the day with fewer ducks than I had seen him shoot. It was a couple of seasons before I learnt that the dog regarded it as his right to eat the first duck of the day and the owner had grown to accept this. We never lay close on the saltings but on a few occasions I noticed the dog lie down on the far side of a creek while returning from a retrieve, presumably for a quick snack. I never felt free to discuss it but I imagine its appetite was a bit sharper than usual and a second duck was following the first. The most practical relationship I know is that of a Hampshire farmer friend, who was one of the Guns on the grouse moor in Chapter 7 and who owns a yellow labrador. The bedrooms of the old Yorkshire pub in which we stayed could be very chilly in the autumn and he took his dog to bed as a canine hot-water bottle.

It is only of late that I have fully appreciated the extent to which dogs develop the personality of their owners. I had long realized that bad-tempered men produce bad-tempered dogs and that it was no coincidence that quiet gentle men own dogs of like natures. These are obvious characteristics but I believe that the similarities run much deeper. A tenacious man who will simply not leave a runner until it is recovered will develop a determined dog and a man who is easily excited will produce a barking, leaping fool of a beast. This is all logical and acceptable but a nasty, prickly suspicion is looming in my mind that whilst dogs grow to behave like their owners, the owners grow to look like their dogs. In fact, had I the courage to publish the evidence I could prove the point by sorting through my collection of photographs. There are angular spinsters with mean-looking retrievers; jolly, round farmers with jolly, round labradors; immaculate and dignified Guns with equally snooty dogs; scruffy men with scruffy dogs and a perky little keeper with a perky little Jack Russell. I am glad I keep springers and not German short-haired pointers.

The first words of this chapter were written on Skye in early September and an experience with my own springer at that time provides a fitting ending. On the last night, when we should have been packing for the journey home, I rebelled and took my sons to a field of oats to which I suspected the mallard would flight at dusk. The springer was tired after a long day seeking grouse on the high ground and when she started to leave the car I sent her back. She looked at me sorrowfully with her big, soft eyes and I said we could manage without her. We spread along the edge of the field and lay in the long grasses while the blues and violets of a Hebridean dusk formed. In time the duck came like big black moths and when the flight was over we had four down in the oats, one a runner. It was very dark and a human retrieve quite impossible. I sent a boy for the spaniel and in a few minutes, without fuss or harm to the corn, we had all four mallard. We returned to the car, switched on the interior light, and she jumped in. I laid the mallard beside her, fondled her head and apologized.

The dogs of my acquaintance are a very mixed bunch but there are very few among them that display any bad characteristics and not one that does not worship its owner. We humans take their existence and devotion too much for granted, as we do so many other good and simple things.

INDEX